U.S.–China Relations in the Twenty-First Century

U.S.–China Relations in the Twenty-First Century

Policies, Prospects, and Possibilities

Edited by Christopher Marsh
and June Teufel Dreyer

LEXINGTON BOOKS
Lanham • Boulder • New York • Oxford

LEXINGTON BOOKS

Published in the United States of America
by Lexington Books
An imprint of The Rowman & Littlefield Publishing Group, Inc.
4501 Forbes Boulevard, Suite 200, Lanham, Maryland 20706

PO Box 317
Oxford
OX2 9RU, UK

British Library Cataloguing in Publication Information Available

Library of Congress Cataloging-in-Publication Data

U.S.–China Relations in the Twenty-First Century: Policies, Prospects,
and Possibilities/edited by Christopher Marsh and June Teufel Dreyer.
    p. cm.
Includes bibliographical references and index.
  ISBN 0-7391-0681-3 (hardcover: alk. paper)—ISBN 0-7391-0682-1
(pbk.: alk. paper)
  1. United States—Foreign relations—China. 2. China—Foreign
relations—United States. 3. United States—Foreign relations—2001–
I. Title: U.S.–China relations in the Twenty-First Century. II. Marsh,
Christopher, 1969– III. Dreyer, June Teufel, 1939–
  E183.8.C5U23 2003
  327.73051—dc21

                                   2003012883

∞™ The paper used in this publication meets the minimum requirements of American
National Standard for Information Sciences—Permanence of Paper for Printed Library
Materials, ANSI/NISO Z39.48–1992.

Contents

Acknowledgments

The current volume is largely the end result of Baylor University's 2002 President's Forum which was held on October 23, 2002 on the eve of the Bush–Jiang Summit at the Prairie Chapel Ranch in Crawford, Texas. The forum brought together participants from across the United States and from a variety of professional fields, including academia and government service. This diverse mix engendered a lively and spirited dialogue. We only hope that we have done an adequate job in putting into book form the ideas and dynamic discussion in which we participated during what was a very enjoyable occasion.

We all owe a debt of gratitude to the divisions of Baylor University that made the symposium possible. This includes the Office of the President, the College of Arts and Sciences, the Office of Public Affairs, and the Asian Studies program. In particular, thanks to President Robert Sloan, Vice President Donald Schmeltekopf, and Dean Wallace Daniel, for making the forum possible. Thanks go especially to James Odom, Director of Public Affairs, for his work on the project from conception to publication, and to his assistant, Ms. Carla Gibbs. For the cover design, thanks to Creative Services in the Office of Public Relations at Baylor University.

A special word of thanks goes to Justin Miller for his excellent work in editing the contributions and compiling the appendix. Thanks also to Jue Sun, Eka Akobia, Jake Podewils, and Mitch Martzen for their assistance during the forum. Thanks also to the *Journal of Democracy* for permission to republish Andrew Nathan's contribution to this volume. Finally, thanks to Serena Krombach at Lexington Books for her useful ideas and help in seeing this project through to publication.

Christopher Marsh
June Teufel Dreyer
April 2003

Introduction

U.S.–China Relations in the Twenty-First Century

Christopher Marsh and June Teufel Dreyer

It has become a cliché to say that the landscape of international relations was fundamentally altered by the events of September 11, 2001. One area which has seen particularly dramatic changes due to the events of that day is the U.S.–China bilateral relationship.[1] Today, pronouncements of a coming conflict with China, so popular just a few years ago, have become muted as both the United States and China face new and unanticipated challenges in the twenty-first century. The United States is in the midst of a battle to ensure its domestic tranquility in the face of terrorism and to make the world safe from those that threaten the use of weapons of mass destruction. China faces challenges of its own and may feel threatened by an increased U.S. military presence in Central Asia and by the war with Iraq. The potential and motivation therefore exists for both countries—the world's most powerful nation and the world's most populous nation—to find ways to cooperate and to pursue mutually advantageous objectives.

The October 2002 meeting of U.S. President George W. Bush and Chinese President Jiang Zemin in Crawford, Texas, provides a fitting juncture to reflect upon the future course of relations between these two nations. In particular, the nature of the changes that have taken place within China over the past two decades, including the trajectory and implications of these changes, must be considered in any assessment of either the future of China or the future of U.S.–China relations. China has made considerable progress in the post-Mao era in the areas of economic, social, and political liberalization, and today is in the midst of an extremely significant leadership transition as the fourth generation of leaders takes the helm of the Middle Kingdom. These factors make this an opportune moment to reflect upon the way in which these changes will likely affect China's behavior in the international system. This knowledge may then be used to promote peace and to facilitate cooperation between our nations.

On October 23, 2002, the eve of Chinese President Jiang Zemin's visit to U.S. President George W. Bush's Crawford ranch, Baylor University held its annual President's Forum. Appropriately, the assembly took U.S.–China relations as its theme, hoping to stimulate a conversation on the future of the Sino–American relationship and to generate insights that will lead to greater mutual understanding and well-informed policy. The forum brought together some of the most astute minds on Chinese affairs and U.S. foreign policy, including Strobe Talbott, former U.S. deputy secretary of state, and J. Stapleton Roy, former U.S. ambassador to China. This volume represents an effort to share some of the conclusions and ideas generated during the forum with the larger academic and policy-making community.

In the chapters that follow, the contributors discuss some of the most critical issues in contemporary U.S.–China relations, as well as provide the necessary background for viewing these issues within a proper historical and cultural perspective. The topics covered range from the sources of the shift in U.S. attitudes toward China from the Clinton to the Bush administration to the implications of China's leadership transition for Chinese foreign policy. In the process, the authors consider the importance of every major development in U.S.–China relations over the past several years, from the success of Chinese economic reform and the rise of civil society to the EP-3 collision and the Taiwan Strait issue. While not all contributors hold the same interpretation of such events or agree on their implications, this volume provides a balanced, nonpartisan account that presents the reader with a brief but comprehensive summary of the issues that are at the forefront of the debate over the future of U.S.–China relations in the twenty-first century.

Following this brief introduction, in which we explore the role of the Crawford ranch in U.S. foreign policy, chapter 1 continues with some thoughts on U.S.–China relations by Strobe Talbott. Mr. Talbott places U.S.–China relations into a historical and global context by summarizing Sino–American relations in the twentieth century and discussing how relations between the two countries were inextricably entwined with trilateral relations involving both countries and the Soviet Union.

In chapter 2, Andrew Nathan considers the resilience of the current regime in Beijing, arguing that Chinese Communist Party (CCP) rule is becoming institutionalized with the transition to the fourth generation. In so doing, he develops a framework for understanding China—not as a communist system doomed to collapse, but one making a transition to a "normal" authoritarian system and perhaps likely to be around for a while. Nathan examines the increasingly norm-bound nature of Chinese leadership succession and the meritocratic nature of political promotion. He also discusses the differentiation and functional specialization of institutions within the regime and the opportunities for political participation that are strengthening the CCP's legitimacy among the public at large. While Nathan does not suggest that these developments guarantee that the regime will be able to solve the challenges it is likely to face, he cautions us against concluding too-hastily that it cannot adapt and survive.

In chapter 3, Carol Lee Hamrin takes a look at the social revolution underway in China. She argues that an unintended consequence of the rapid economic growth engendered by policies introduced by party and government has been a wholesale social transformation. Hamrin argues that this transformation will be central in shaping the China of the future, as rapid social and cultural changes now underway will force the country's new leadership to revise its current reactionary social and religious policies. In the end, party and state will abandon their totalistic aspirations and negative view of religion. Hamrin concludes by arguing that China's social problems are the Achilles' heel of the regime, and that these problems are of tremendous importance to the United States, for it is an area rife with bilateral friction over religious and other human rights.

In chapter 4, Minxin Pei focuses on the domestic changes underway in China more broadly, and takes stock of the successes and failures U.S. policy has had in encouraging the emergence of democratic political institutions in the world's largest authoritarian regime. He warns that short-term skepticism about the feasibility of China's democratic transformation should not be grounds for abandoning such an objective. In fact, Pei argues that American engagement with China over the last thirty years has created an international environment extremely conducive to China's undertaking significant social, economic, and political reform. He concludes by probing the implications of China's domestic reforms for U.S. policy.

Suisheng Zhao examines the rise of Chinese nationalism in chapter 5. Zhao argues that as faith in communism declined in post-Tiananmen China, the CCP rediscovered the utility of nationalism. Today, nationalism is not only openly promoted by the communist state, but also advocated by many Chinese intellectuals. It is even reflected in the popular mood. The foreign policy implications of Chinese nationalism are still unclear, Zhao contends, for although it has not yet transformed into an irrational and aggressive nationalism tied to a confrontational foreign policy stance, China's pragmatic leaders are in danger of falling victim to the nationalism that they themselves have cultivated. In this case, Chinese foreign policy could be dictated by the emotional voice of university students and liberal nationalist intellectuals.

June Teufel Dreyer looks in depth at national security issues in chapter 6. She notes that, because of the People's Republic of China's (PRC) initial military weakness, its leadership has historically been concerned with preventing China from being encircled by powers regarded as hostile to it. In the 1970s and 1980s, Beijing was quite successful in playing the Soviet Union and the United States against each another, to China's benefit. After the disintegration of the USSR in 1991, this was no longer possible, and Beijing sought to create a countervailing coalition to offset the power of what it perceived as Washington's now unrestrained ambitions to play the role of global hegemon. Although these efforts yielded some gains for Beijing's international position, they were sharply set back by events set in motion by terrorist attacks on the World Trade Center and Pentagon in September 2001.

J. Stapleton Roy concludes the volume by discussing the challenges and opportunities in U.S.–China relations. He judges the emergence of the PRC as a stronger and prosperous country to be far more significant than terrorism in determining the peace and stability of Asia and, in fact, of the world. After briefly summarizing tensions within the Sino-American relationship, Roy notes that, although it has not been possible to solve these problems, we have been able to keep them from blocking cooperation between our two countries. Nonetheless, the future of U.S.–China relations remains uncertain.

THE WESTERN WHITE HOUSE
AND EAST–WEST RELATIONS

Before delving into the myriad issues that confound and complicate relations between the United States and China, it is important to first place into context the particular event that brought the contributors to this volume together and which served as both an intellectual and physical background this conversation—the October 25, 2002 summit between U.S. President George W. Bush and Chinese President Jiang Zemin at Bush's Prairie Chapel Ranch in Crawford, Texas. One distinctive feature of this summit is that it was held in central Texas at the president's home, rather than in a more traditional venue. George W. Bush is not the first president to use his vacation home for diplomatic purposes, however, and in fact presidents from at least Eisenhower on have entertained foreign dignitaries in this way.

The best-known holiday site for the American president to host foreign dignitaries is, of course, the presidential retreat at Camp David, named by President Dwight Eisenhower in honor of his new grandson. Over the years, the facility has been used for such historic events as Eisenhower's meetings with French president Charles DeGaulle and Soviet leader Nikita Khrushchev. At a later date,

President Richard Nixon hosted Khrushchev's successor, Leonid Brezhnev, at Camp David. While probably best known as the site of President Jimmy Carter's eponymous Camp David Agreement, the compound has also played an important diplomatic role since that time. Among other notable visitors to the Maryland compound are Soviet General Secretary Mikhail Gorbachev, who was hosted by President George Bush the elder; Israeli Prime Minister Ehud Barak, who met with President Bill Clinton; and British Prime Minister Tony Blair, who appeared there at the invitation of the younger President Bush.

While Camp David is a retreat, most presidents have also had their own real vacation hideaways, with New England being a particular favorite. President Kennedy spent his free time in Hyannisport; President Bush the elder chose Kennebunkport for his vacations; and President Clinton enjoyed golfing and relaxing at Martha's Vineyard. The true parallel for the Crawford ranch, however, takes us back to another Texan president, Lyndon Baines Johnson, more colloquially known as "LBJ." President Johnson hosted foreign dignitaries at his home while still a congressional leader but, after assuming office, he converted his ranch into what the press referred to as the "Texas White House." Among the guests who appeared there were Chancellor Ludwig Erhard of Germany, President Gustavo Diaz Ordaz of Mexico, and President Levi Eshkol of Israel.

While it might seem that Bush is following in the tradition of LBJ by using his Texas ranch as a vacation spot and diplomatic tool, Bush has been more selective in his choice of guests. The first high-level visitor to the ranch was Russian President Vladimir Putin, who visited in November of 2001. This meeting was a follow-up to the first Bush–Putin Summit held in Slovenia in June 2001, where the two leaders began to develop a relationship of mutual trust. It was at this meeting that Bush invited Putin to his ranch. Following the September 11 attacks, the relationship between Bush and Putin grew even stronger. Immediately after hearing of the tragedy, Putin placed a call to President Bush to express his sympathy, becoming the first world leader to do so.

After Putin's visit to the Crawford ranch, other foreign dignitaries have had the distinction of being invited to Crawford, including Saudi Crown Prince Abdullah, British Prime Minister Tony Blair, and Mexican President Vicente Fox, whose own ranch President Bush had visited in February 2001. Fox never made his scheduled visit to the ranch in August 2002, however, as he felt compelled to cancel his visit after the United States executed a convicted police killer, Javier Suarez Medina. The controversy surrounding this execution relates to Suarez's citizenship, with Fox maintaining that he was a Mexican national and should have been tried in Mexico, while Texas officials stated that it was unclear on which side of the border Suarez was born.

The fact that President Fox never visited the ranch means that Jiang Zemin was only the fourth foreign leader hosted by President Bush at the Crawford ranch. If we look at his three predecessors, a pattern emerges. Crown Prince Abdullah of Saudi Arabia and British Prime Minister Tony Blair represent some of America's closest allies, particularly with regard to the war on terrorism. President Fox's invitation to the ranch can be seen in these terms as well: U.S.–Mexico relations are vital to the success of the war on terrorism, particularly with respect to the Narcoterrorist nexus. The decision to host these foreign leaders at Bush's ranch should therefore be seen as more than mere diplomatic socializing. Such invitations are in essence strategic moves to strengthen relations with America's most important allies.

This pattern is confirmed by Putin's visit to the ranch. In this case the Bush–Putin Summit in Crawford was an important stage in the process of turning Russia into an ally. While it is true that U.S.–Russia relations were good during the 1990s, due in no small part to the role played by one of the contributors to this volume, Strobe Talbott, U.S.–Russia relations were consistently somewhat strained during this period due to the war in Chechnya and the human rights violations there and the shaky nature of Russian democracy. In the post-Yeltsin period, many American policy makers and academics felt somewhat uneasy regarding Putin's rapid rise to power and his swift moves to clamp down on the media and address the Chechnya situation with renewed vigor.

It is therefore somewhat surprising that Bush and Putin developed such warm relations so quickly. To understand this phenomenon, we must consider the fact that Bush received a very cold welcome during his first visit to Europe in the spring of 2001. In June, however, Putin extended the hand of friendship to Bush, and the two seemed very impressed by each another. It was the September 11 terrorist attacks, however, that brought the two even closer together. Putin not only gave Bush his sympathy, he made a huge concession by allowing U.S. forces to operate in Russia's backyard in Central Asia. This friendship has not stopped Putin from denouncing U.S. actions in Iraq nor did it prevent the Russian Federal Assembly from tabling ratification of the Treaty of Moscow, a significant agreement on U.S. and Russian reductions in offensive nuclear weapons whose terms were largely reached at the ranch. Nevertheless, the Bush–Putin Summit of November 2001 was a major step in bringing Russia on board as an ally in the war on terrorism.

The prior history of Bush's Western White House thus leads us to conclude that, as a senior member of his administration remarked, "Crawford is for friends." Indeed, this is exactly what Jiang and others had surmised, and is the reason they began to approach the topic of a visit to the ranch through back channels during the spring following Bush's February 2002 visit to the PRC. Bush's visit was itself highly symbolic, since it marked thirty years to the day since Richard Nixon had visited China and met with Chairman Mao Zedong, becoming the first U.S. president to visit the People's Republic. Nixon's visit inaugurated a new and less confrontational era in U.S.–China relations. Bush's visit had the potential to foster improved relations between the United States and the PRC. In contrast to his meetings with Putin and Blair, however, Bush's meeting with Jiang Zemin did not result in an invitation to Crawford.

While Jiang may initially have felt somewhat slighted by not being invited to the ranch, he later appeared to become fixated on the idea, perhaps viewing it as the perfect capstone to his presidency. Possibly he viewed it as a tool to show how indispensable he was for China and thus to help him hold onto positions of influence in the Chinese government. This may explain why the Sixteenth Congress of the Chinese Communist Party, an event typically held in September or October, was postponed until after Jiang's visit to the United States, so that he would remain the unquestioned leader of China during his visit. While this is all a matter of speculation, it is a fact that Jiang was so dedicated to the idea that he sent an advance team to Crawford to check on the logistics of such a visit. Somewhat embarrassingly, team members were stopped by the Crawford police, since they had neither asked for nor received permission to explore the well-guarded property and its surroundings.[2]

The Bush–Jiang Summit was more than simply a capstone to the Jiang presidency. It became an important step in improving U.S.–China relations and epitomized the mutual desire for better understanding between the two nations. On the U.S. side, Jiang's visit brought the Middle Kingdom center stage in the American media and increased American awareness of China and its current situation. On the other side of the Pacific Ocean, most Chinese considered it a very symbolic gesture for President Bush to welcome the Chinese leader to his home. Perhaps also this event helped repair some of the damage caused by such incidents as the bombing of the Chinese Embassy in Belgrade in May 1999 and the collision of a U.S. EP-3 surveillance plane with a Chinese fighter jet in April 2001. All of these events, of course, occurred prior to the September 11 attacks. Since that time the United States and China seem to have become less concerned with the strategic threat they pose to each other and more concerned with the war on terrorism and China's leadership succession. This focus on the symbolic significance of the Bush–Jiang Summit, however, should not obscure the strategic importance of this event. Jiang's visit to Crawford was an opportunity, not an answer. As discussed in the following chapters, there are numerous issues that will continue to plague U.S.–China relations far into the future.

NOTES

1. An excellent early account of these changes is found in David M. Lampton and Richard D. Ewing, *U.S.–China Relations in a Post–September 11th World* (Washington, D.C.: Nixon Center, 2002). See also Michael Swaine and Minxin Pei, "Rebalancing United States–China Relations," Policy Brief 13 (February 2002), Washington, D.C.: Carnegie Endowment for International Peace.

2. Author's conversation with members of the Crawford Police Department, July 2002.

1

U.S.–China Relations in a Changing World

Strobe Talbott

During a recent trip to Beijing, I met with a number of officials, most of whom I had known and worked with when I was part of the U.S. government. I found all of these meetings to be extremely upbeat, largely because my Chinese hosts wanted to underscore what good shape U.S.–China relations are in, which by the way, is not always the message that they wanted to convey to me when I was traveling there as a representative of the U.S. government. One reason they wanted to put a very positive spin on this relationship is because they wanted to create the best possible atmosphere for the Crawford Summit. They are acutely aware of the symbolic importance of the fact that President Jiang Zemin has been invited to President Bush's ranch. They know that this is not a courtesy that President Bush provides to all his foreign interlocutors, and that by going to Crawford President Jiang Zemin is joining the company of what might be called "special friends" of the United States and of its president. That group includes Crown Prince Abdullah of Saudi Arabia, Prime Minister Tony Blair of the United Kingdom, and of course Vladimir Putin, who was a guest at the ranch in Crawford in November 2001.

In Beijing, I found that the Chinese officials had kept score on exactly what symbols were made public, of the good relations between the United States and Russia, and that they were hoping for similar symbols when President Jiang went to the ranch himself. One of the officials jokingly said that he had asked the Chinese advance party to make sure that the American presidential authorities knew exactly what were President Jiang's hat size and boot size. Just beneath the surface of all of this very sincere good will and high hopes, however, there was deep seriousness, and even some concerns on two fronts. One was the near-term relationship between the United States and China, particularly regarding Iraq and the probability of another war in the Gulf. They also had some concerns about the long term, which is to say about the strategic direction of U.S.–China relations.

The Chinese are the custodians of a continuous civilization of over 4,000 years' standing, and they like to remind us that just as they have a long view looking backward, they also take a long view looking forward. I remember the first trip I made to China. As a reporter, for many years I covered Dr. Kissinger when he was both national security advisor and secretary of state, and I accompanied him to China in 1975. This was one of the first trips that he made that he actually allowed what the Chinese in those days called "the running dogs of the bourgeois capitalist press" to fly with him on his plane. On our way home, I remember Dr. Kissinger remarking to those of us reporters traveling with him that he had the following exchange with Zhao Enlai. Dr. Kissinger asked if in Zhao Enlai's view the French Revolution had benefited humanity, to which after thinking for a moment Zhao Enlai replied, "It's too soon to tell."

I think there is some contrast here between the Chinese preference for the long view and the penchant for impatience that we Americans tend to have. That is not entirely surprising, culturally or historically. After all, the United States has been around as a state for one-twentieth as long as China. Also, the United States is prone to mood swings, particularly with regards to former adversaries that also happen to be very large and complex countries. Here, of course, our principal examples are Russia and China.

There is no question that we are currently in a period when the mood is good. Despite the basically favorable state of U.S.–China relations at present, that relationship has yet to be firmly grounded in a concept and a strategy for the long haul, at least on the American side. In fact, it has never been firmly grounded in a coherent, long-term analysis or strategy (that does not mean that there are not individuals who have brought that kind of coherence to the issue). Official U.S. policy toward China has been too dependent on exogenous and unpredictable events, hence the kind of "pendulum swinging back and forth" quality that the relationship has sometimes had. What is needed is for the United States to fix public attitudes toward China over time. I will try to illustrate that point with reference to recent history, and then suggest a way of thinking about China that is perhaps more appropriate, not only to the need for continuity in the relationship, but also suitable to the ways in which the world is changing. This point also applies to Russia. Incidentally, I will keep bringing Russia back into this conversation, not just because Russia has been my own professional preoccupation in the several careers that I have had, but because there really is an important link between Russia and China. These are giant countries, after all, respectively the largest countries on earth in terms of land mass (Russia) and population (China), and they are neighbors that dominate the double continent of Eurasia.

U.S.–CHINA RELATIONS
IN THE TWENTIETH CENTURY

Although our topic is U.S.–China relations in the twenty-first century, it is worth looking back at the relationship in the twentieth century. For a quarter of a century, after the birth of the People's Republic of China (PRC), that country's relationship with the United States was one of the most antagonistic on the face of the earth, and one of the most antagonistic in history. It rivaled in antagonism quotient the relationship between the United States and a country that no longer exists, the Union of Soviet Socialist Republics (USSR). While all are aware that there was a cold war in Europe, much less is understood about the cold war in Asia, where there was a "bamboo curtain" instead of an "iron curtain." And unlike the cold war in Europe, the cold war in Asia actually turned hot on several occasions, bringing the United States and China into direct military conflict with each other, both directly on the Korean Peninsula and by proxy in Indochina. In fact, it is accurate to say that in some way to many Americans, China was seen as being even more sinister, even more dangerous than the Soviet Union. This was perhaps partly because there was more mystery associated with China; we simply did not understand it that well. There was no diplomatic relationship between the United States and China during that period, whereas, of course, there was between the United States and the Soviet Union even in the depths of the Cold War. Also, there was the fact that Mao Zedong presided in the 1950s and 1960s over the carnage and slaughter of his own people under the banners of the Great Leap Forward and the Great Proletarian Cultural Revolution. These events were even more recent and therefore more immediate for many of us than Stalin's meat grinder of the purges of the 1930s.

For all of these reasons, China was seen as even more of a villain and an enemy than was the Soviet Union. In fact, back in the 1960s it was often said that the optimists were learning to speak Russian and the pessimists were learning to speak Chinese. I guess having studied Russian made me an optimist, at least at that time. The point that must be stressed here is that the conventional wisdom for a very long period of time in our country was that the USSR and the PRC were the evil twins of this great twilight struggle with the United States, and that those two huge countries were essentially a single, hostile predatory conglomerate.

Then something extraordinary happened in the 1960s. All of the sudden we came to the realization—and we were collectively a little slow to fully realize this—that the Soviet Union and China did not constitute a monolith. In fact, they were at each other's throats in many ways. In quite a short period of time we went from talking about the Sino–Soviet camp to talking about the Sino–Soviet schism or split. And then on March 2, 1969, fighting broke out between Soviet and Chinese troops over Damansky (Chen Pao) Island in the Ussuri River. Fighting continued on into the summer over this and other islands as well as some largely unpopulated terrain along the Amur and Ussuri rivers that constituted the border between the Soviet Union and China.[1] During the crisis, in one of the more amazing incidents in Cold War history, the Brezhnev regime actually sent a signal to the Nixon administration asking if the United States would tolerate—and perhaps even welcome—a Soviet preemptive strike against the Chinese nuclear facilities, resulting in an early version of a preemptive doctrine.[2]

What lay behind this amazing overture that Brezhnev made to President Nixon was the hope that the United States would make a common cause with the Soviet Union against China. The United States, and President Nixon in particular, had a better idea, which was that the United States and China would make common cause against the Soviet Union. This position was based on the belief that the Soviets were more aggressive, particularly in the geographical framework of Europe, which is to say in a way that threatened the vital allies of the United States. This idea of a common cause between Washington and Beijing very much suited Mao Zedong because he felt betrayed by the Soviets and in some ways threatened by them himself. That, of course, led to the U.S.–China opening.

The point that needs to be stressed here is that the U.S.–China–Soviet triangular relationship was a classic example of what might be considered *classical geopolitics*. By this phrase I mean that international relations are dominated by rivalries, antagonisms, and for that matter, realignments and alliances of convenience between and among states. Geopolitics is based on the principle that the nineteenth-century British Foreign Secretary Lord Palmerston summarized when he said, "there are no permanent alliances, only permanent interests." It is also summed up by that phrase which I am told has its origins appropriately enough in the Middle East, "the enemy of my enemy is my friend." In that sense, China became a strategic collaborator of convenience for the United States as a result of the enmity between the United States and the Soviet Union and the enmity between China and the Soviet Union. It took several years, of course, to develop and grow into fully normalized relations, only reaching full normalization under the Carter administration.

Normalization between the United States and China was not easy, because it meant that the United States along with China had to finesse a couple of very tough issues: Taiwan, which was governed by anti-Communists but claimed by Beijing; and ideology, which is to say the nature of the Chinese system, which after all remained very much a Communist dictatorship during this period. The Taiwan situation was dealt with by the Shanghai Communiqué and some additional agreements that ratified and elaborated upon the essential terms of the Shanghai Communiqué. The essence of the policy was—and remains today—that there is one China, and that the difficulties between Taiwan and the PRC must be solved peacefully. That leaves plenty of details where the devil resides, but that was the essence of the way in which the Taiwan issue was handled.

Ideology was finessed by the concept of engagement, which meant that rather than confronting China and containing China, what we should do was try to coax the Chinese toward the eventual realization that ours was a better system, a better way of governing a country and a better way of getting along with the world. That policy or concept of engagement was encouraged by what was going on in China following the death of Mao Zedong in 1976 and the almost immediate purge of the Gang of Four. It was the rise of Deng Xiaoping and his pragmatic, quasi-capitalist reforms that modernized the economy, introduced the principles of the market at home, and opened China to the world. The theory that guided our side, and the reason that we could welcome these changes and fit them into a framework of engagement as a way of handling the ideological dispute between us, was that we felt correctly then, and I feel correctly now, that economic liberalization would over time be conducive to political liberalization.

U.S.–CHINA RELATIONS AFTER MAO

The period of China's opening was an extraordinary time. Virtually overnight, any echoes of the "who lost China" accusations and debate disappeared into the past, and the United States all of a sudden seemed to be having a kind of love affair with all things Chinese. So-called China-bashers went out of fashion, and the so-called panda-huggers were back in fashion for the first time since the birth of the People's Republic. Of course, that did not last. This related back to my earlier point about mood swings, because in the late 1980s and 1990s there were three developments that threw a monkey wrench into what otherwise might have been a steady, affirmative development of U.S.–China relations.

One of those developments was, quite simply, the collapse of the USSR. Democracy came to the Soviet Union—a messy, primitive, incomplete democracy, but a democracy nonetheless—and the Cold War came to an end. That development undermined the strategic rationale for U.S.–China protocol, and it undermined it on both sides, because now the United States, rather than having an interest in containing and counterbalancing the old USSR, had an interest in supporting reform in Russia. There was, of course, as there always is, a personal dimension to the shift that occurred, as Mikhail Gorbachev became the darling of the United States. The shift took place on both sides, and on the China side there was no longer a need to serve as a counterweight to the big, bad polar bear, which is the way the Chinese had tried to depict the Soviet Union.

The second development that fouled things up a bit in the 1980s, particularly in the late 1980s, was that there was blood in the streets of Beijing, and indeed in the streets of other Chinese cities as well. Here the triggering event, or at least one among several triggering events, was the peaceful democratic revolution that had taken place in the Soviet Union.[3] A lot of young Chinese in particular saw what was happening in the Soviet Union and became quite impatient for change and began to challenge their own regime. In Tiananmen Square in the spring of 1989, in addition to the paper mâché, giant replicas of our own Statue of Liberty, there were also banners and posters asking "Where is our Gorbachev?"[4] The answer was that he was not around. The Chinese had Deng Xiaoping and the leadership of the time who sent tanks into Tiananmen, resulting in televised slaughter, martyrs, outrage, and disillusionment in the United States and around the world.

The third complicating factor had to do with Taiwan itself, because the people of Taiwan had become accustomed to its de facto independence. While the United States was sticking to its one-China policy, a lot of Taiwanese politicians began to explicitly proclaim a two-China policy in public, which is to say their de jure independence. Quite expectedly, the reaction from Beijing was one of fury and threats, and statements that they would solve the problem by force, which of course contradicted the principle of peaceful resolution of the issue that had been sanctified in the Shanghai Communiqué and elsewhere. That led to moments of tension, including military tension with the United States.

What this all meant is that when President Clinton came to office U.S.–China relations were pretty rocky. President Clinton came into office talking quite toughly about China and in fact criticizing his predecessor, the first President Bush, as being too soft on China. But rather soon after President Clinton came into office he modulated his policy and began talking about strategic cooperation with the PRC, reiterating the one-China policy with regard to Taiwan, and certainly restoring the importance of engagement as the basis for U.S.–China relations.

Moving on to our current administration and the attitudes and policies of President George W. Bush, at the beginning of his administration President Bush presided over a fairly rocky transition in relations with China. This was partly due to the fact that he had in his team of advisors a number of people who are powerful, combatant intellects who hold a worldview that has tended to target China as the United States' main adversary in the twenty-first century, making China in effect the successor to the Soviet Union in the role that it played in the twentieth century. For example, Deputy Secretary of Defense Paul Wolfowitz said during the presidential campaign, "China is in the process of becoming—albeit still quite slowly—the major strategic competitor and potential threat to the United States and its allies in the first half of the next century."[5] Not long after that, Condoleezza Rice, President George W. Bush's national security advisor, wrote in 2000 that China was a "strategic competitor, not the 'strategic partner' the Clinton administration once called it."[6] When you see a phrase like that—a "strategic competitor"—used twice by two people closely associated with someone who is running for president, it is not usually a coincidence, it is a harbinger of what is likely to be the policy or strategy of the new administration, at least at the outset, and it was certainly seen that way in Beijing.[7] I can also attest to that based upon my own experience. During a trip to China in the spring of last year I heard a number of Chinese officials say that the China-bashers are back. They were particularly distressed, appalled, and surprised because they had such a good relationship with the first President Bush, who had been head of the American foreign liaison office there, and whose own administration had tried to smooth things over during the Tiananmen Crisis. Having only recently left the government and now as a private citizen, I got a real earful, and they would have me believe that relations were heading back into a new cold war in Asia with a potential at least of that war turning hot.

Then there is one of those episodes where things get so bad that it causes them to get better. The collision of a U.S. EP-3 reconnaissance plane with a Chinese fighter jet over the South China Sea on April 1, 2001 was just such an event. That incident seemed to be almost a metaphor for the two giant countries that were suddenly on a collision course, and it was really the first serious crisis for the new Bush administration. The situation was resolved in a mutually advantageous manner, and in fact it had a kind of sobering effect on both sides. It also tipped the balance within the Bush administration in favor of diplomats, led by the diplomatic chief, Secretary of State Colin Powell, vis-à-vis what you might call the fire breathers, who were in effect looking for a new fight and a new enemy, a group that tended to be concentrated more on the civilian side of the upper levels of the civilian leadership of the Department of Defense.

THE CRAWFORD SUMMIT AND THE
FUTURE OF U.S.–CHINA RELATIONS

These events bring us into the twenty-first century and then to September 11, 2001. It has become a great cliché to say that September 11 was a transforming event in international relations, but in many ways it was, notably including its effect on U.S.–China relations. What happened quite simply was that those in the U.S. administration who were looking for a new enemy to replace the USSR no longer had to search. They had one, and the new enemy was global terrorism. It was in that context that President Bush proclaimed, "if you are not with us, you are against us" in the fight against global terrorism. China was very quick to answer "we are with you." One reason they were quick to answer that way is that the Chinese have what they regard as their own terrorism problem. It is focused on the Xinjiang Uygur Autonomous Region, where there is a Muslim, Turkic-speaking ethnic minority. When the United States heard this response from the Chinese, the United States said to the Chinese, "We are with you, too." In other words, the Bush Administration decided to extend its own counterterrorism policy to the case of the Xinjiang, and to designate the separatists in the Xinjiang province as a terrorist organization. So for the second time in thirty years, China went from being a potential enemy to being an enemy of our enemy, and therefore our friend.

That friendship became personalized in the relationship that developed between President Jiang and President Bush to the point that we now have the third summit meeting between the two of them in less than a year. It is not just a matter of atmospherics and of cowboy hats. In addition to cooperation on terror, these two leaders and the two governments have a great deal of common business that they want to do together. This includes rebuilding Afghanistan, a country that is physically contiguous with China; coordinating diplomacy in South Asia, which is to say trying to keep India and Pakistan from going to nuclear war over Kashmir; and then there is the issue that has been in the headlines so much recently, which is peace or war on the Korean Peninsula.

Despite the fact that both the atmospherics and the substantive agenda are somewhat positive, it would be premature and probably foolish to count on a bright future for U.S.–China relations. A number of the fundamental problems persist, notably including that of Taiwan. President Jiang Zemin is likely to push President Bush in private on clarification on where he personally stands on the question of Taiwan, to make sure that there is no departure from the One-China policy of previous administrations. Nor, by the way, are the

Chinese convinced that the Bush administration has given up entirely on the notion of China as a long-term rival of the United States. I heard a lot about this during my recent trip to Beijing. With regards to the Bush doctrine that was released on September 20, 2002, about eight of the people I met in Beijing had read every single one of the 13,000 words in that document very carefully, underlining it (and showing me their underlining!), and wanting to parse individual phrases.

On the one hand, there were parts of the document that they tended to welcome. For example, they were glad that it spoke positively about the emergence of a strong, peaceful, prosperous China. I would say their overall reaction was quite cautious, however, and even suspicious. I think that a number of them feel that the mild talk, even the encouraging talk, about U.S.–China relations in the document was motivated more by tactical convenience by September 11 than by real strategic commitment. For example, they all emphasized that it was more important in a way than anything else in the document that the national security strategy reiterated the administration's assertion that the United States will never permit another power to challenge American military supremacy or predominance. The quote that they had highlighted reads as follows: "Our forces will be strong enough to persuade potential adversaries from pursuing a military buildup in the hopes of surpassing or equaling the power of the United States." I can assure you that the Chinese have every intention of being a major military power in East Asia. They are not about to acquiesce to the idea that the Pacific should remain—in the phrase that a Chinese general I met with used—"an American lake." The question, therefore, is how do we avoid returning to a collision course when we move, as we all pray that we will, into the *post*–post-September 11 era and we are back once again to dealing with relations in their own terms rather than in the context of "the enemy of my enemy is my friend?"

We need to make the most of the changing context of international relations. The old context emphasized interests and official interactions—whether they be cooperative or conflictual—and the prerogatives of nation–states, of these entities which are color coded on the map and have capitals and names and seats in the United Nations. The old context relied almost exclusively on the interaction of the major powers. That is the image that is brought to mind when I hear the phrase geopolitics. It is a world in which interactions among the great powers are constantly shifting in a zero-sum game, and all of the pieces on the grand chess board, from pawns all the way up to kings and queens, are states.

What is the new context? How has that changed? I think that what has happened is that we now have the makings of a new international system, for better or for worse. We all have to make sure that it is for the better. I think that classical geopolitics of the variety just described is gradually being at least complicated, and perhaps ultimately replaced, by what I would call global politics. The differences between *geopolitics* and *global politics* are many. *Geopolitics* means state-to-state relations, states versus states, states aligned with states. Those are the relationships that are considered to matter. *Global politics* implies that there are forces, factors, and actors that operate independently of states, often in defiance of states and in disregard of their rules and borders. They become new forces to contend with, new enemies that require alliances and coalitions of states across international lines. We now have this whole new species of actors on the world stage that are substate, crossstate, and transstate rather than national. To return to the chess metaphor, it is now as though there are a lot of pawns that are moving independently of states, and the prime example is, of course, terrorism and terrorist networks. In this sense, Al Qaeda in some ways is the ultimate nongovernmental organization (NGO). It has, of course, found refuge in states, but it does not play by the rules or follow the behavior of states. Another example is the proliferation of weapons of mass destruction. Then, of course, you have environmental degradation, whose causes and effects are transnational and not something that states can control. And, of course, there is the gruesome example of epidemics like HIV.

In addition to the problem of non-state actors, there are states that operate in flagrant violation of the emerging rules of the game, by which I mean the rules of what is becoming not just the international community but the human community. These are rogue states, which operate on the chess board as knights, bishops, and rooks. Here I am referring to countries like North Korea and Iraq.

THE CHALLENGES AHEAD

The United States, China, and Russia are three powers that, at the second half of the twentieth century, participated in a deadly dance of triangular rivalry based on geopolitics and ideology. The ideological argument is essentially over, and geopolitics is being eroded by the forces of globalization, both positive and negative. Global politics are asserting themselves as a competing factor for the old geopolitics. Moreover, Russia, China, and the United States constitute three of the five permanent members of the United Nations Security Council, and the question is: can these three countries, given their power, prestige, and institutional position recognize the shift that has taken place and make it work in the transformation from a zero-sum game to a win-win game among themselves and the world in coping with these big problems?

All of that, I would suggest, is the backdrop to the Crawford Summit. President Bush and President Jiang are meeting in a time of triple crisis. First, there is the war on terrorism, and that is far from over. Osama bin Laden is apparently still out there, and Al Qaeda is down but not out. Second, the United States might be on the brink of war, and it is looking for Chinese support for that war in the United Nations. Meanwhile, North Korea has challenged the world, including its own neighbors, by declaring its determination to acquire nuclear weapons.

There was something else that Zhou Enlai said to Henry Kissinger in 1975 that he thought significant enough that he passed it on to me and to other members of the press corps. Zhou Enlai pointed out to Dr. Kissinger that the word in Chinese for crisis is *weiji*, which is made up of two characters which mean danger and opportunity, respectively. Now the dangers are all obvious in the crises that I have discussed, but the opportunity is evident, too. I think that they are crystallized—both the danger and the opportunity—in the weeks and days ahead in what we are going to be dealing with over Iraq. If the United States, China, and Russia can work together and remain together in meeting that challenge, then the future is bright. As to whether we will meet that test, I guess all I can say is what Zhou Enlai might have said, "It's too soon to tell."

NOTES

This chapter is an edited version of a keynote address delivered as part of the Baylor University President's Forum, 23 October 2002.

1. An excellent analysis of the events that relies upon recently released secret documents is William Burr, "Sino–American Relations, 1969: The Sino–Soviet Border War and Steps Towards Rapprochement," *Cold War History* 1, 3 (April 2001): 73–112.

2. U.S. State Department Memorandum of Conversation, "U.S. Reaction to Soviet Destruction of CPR [Chinese People's Republic] Nuclear Capability; Significance of Latest Sino–Soviet Border Clash," 18 August 1969, National Archives, SN 67–69, Def 12 Chicom.

3. The impact of Soviet democratization on support for the Chinese reform movement is examined in Christopher Marsh, *Unparalleled Reforms: Lessondrawing and Policy Choice in the Soviet and Chinese Transitions from Communism* (forthcoming).

4. Nicholas Kristof, "China's Hero of Democracy: Gorbachev," *New York Times,* May 14, 1989, 10.

5. Jeff Gerth and Eric Schmitt, "Chinese Said to Reap Gains in U.S. Export Policy Shift," *The New York Times*, October 19, 1998.

6. Condoleezza Rice, "Campaign 2000—Promoting the National Interest," *Foreign Affairs* 79, 1 (January/February 2000).

7. "Bush's Position on America's China Policy is Harmful," *Beijing Review* 42 (October 16, 2000).

2

Authoritarian Resilience: Institutionalization and the Transition to China's Fourth Generation

Andrew J. Nathan

After the Tiananmen Square crisis in June 1989, many observers thought that the rule of the Chinese Communist Party (CCP) would collapse. Instead, the regime brought inflation under control, restarted economic growth, expanded foreign trade, and increased its absorption of foreign direct investment. It restored normal relations with the G-7 countries that had imposed sanctions, resumed the exchange of summits with the United States, presided over the retrocession of Hong Kong to Chinese sovereignty, and won the right to hold the 2008 Olympics in Beijing. It arrested or exiled political dissidents, crushed the fledgling China Democratic Party, and seems to have largely suppressed the Falun Gong spiritual movement.

Many China specialists and democracy theorists—myself among them—expected the regime to fall to democratization's "third wave."[1] Instead, the regime has reconsolidated itself.[2] Regime theory holds that authoritarian systems are inherently fragile because of weak legitimacy, overreliance on coercion, overcentralization of decision making, and the predominance of personal power over institutional norms. This particular authoritarian system, however, has proven resilient.

The causes of its resilience are complex. Many of them, however, can be summed up in the concept of institutionalization—understood either in the currently fashionable sense of behavior that is constrained by formal and informal rules, or in the older sense summarized by Samuel P. Huntington as consisting of the adaptability, complexity, autonomy, and coherence of state organizations.[3] This chapter focuses on four aspects of the CCP regime's institutionalization: first, the increasingly norm-bound nature of its succession politics; second, the increase in meritocratic as opposed to factional considerations in the promotion of political elites; third, the differentiation and functional specialization of institutions within the regime; and fourth, the establishment of institutions for political participation and appeal that strengthen the CCP's legitimacy among the public at large. While these developments do not guarantee that the regime will be able to solve all the challenges that it faces, they do caution against too-hasty arguments that it cannot adapt and survive.

NORM-BOUND SUCCESSION POLITICS

The Chinese regime is in the middle of a historic demonstration of institutional stability: its peaceful, orderly transition from the so-called third generation of leadership, headed by Jiang Zemin, to the fourth, headed by Hu Jintao. Few authoritarian regimes—be they communist, fascist, corporatist, or personalist—have managed to conduct orderly, peaceful, timely, and stable successions. Instead, the moment of transfer has almost always been a moment of crisis—breaking out ahead of or behind the nominal schedule, involving purges or arrests, factionalism, sometimes violence, and opening the door to the chaotic intrusion into the political process of the masses or the military. China's current succession displays attributes of institutionalization unusual in the history of authoritarianism and unprecedented in the history of the PRC. It is the most orderly, peaceful, deliberate, and rule-bound succession in the history of modern China outside of the recent institutionalization of electoral democracy in Taiwan.[4]

Hu Jintao, the new general secretary of the CCP as of the Sixteenth Party Congress in November 2002, has held the position of successor-apparent for ten years. Four of the other eight top-ranking appointments (Wu Bangguo, Wen Jiabao, Zeng Qinghong, and Luo Gan) had been decided a year or two in advance. The remaining four members of the Politburo Standing Committee (PBSC) were simply elevated from the outgoing Politburo. Barring a major crisis, the transition will continue to an orderly conclusion in March 2003, leading to the election of Hu Jintao as state president and chairman of the Central Military Commission, Wu Bangguo as chair of the National People's Congress (NPC), and Wen Jiabao as premier. Outgoing officials President Jiang Zemin, NPC Chair Li Peng, and Premier Zhu Rongji will leave their state offices, having already left their Party offices in the fall, and will cease to have any direct role in politics.

It takes some historical perspective to appreciate this outcome for the achievement that it is. During the Mao years, Party congresses and National People's congresses seldom met, and when they did it was rarely on schedule. There have never before been effective terms of office or age limits for persons holding the rank of "central leader;" Mao and Deng each exercised supreme authority until the end of his life. Nor has there ever been an orderly assumption of office by a designated successor: Mao purged Liu Shaoqi, the president of the PRC, by having Red Guards seize him and put him in prison, where he died. Mao's officially designated successor, Lin Biao, allegedly tried to seize power from Mao, was discovered, and died in a plane crash while fleeing. Mao appointed Hua Guofeng as his successor simply by stating that Hua was his choice. Hua was removed from office at Deng Xiaoping's behest before Hua's term of office was over. Deng removed from power both of his own chosen successors, Hu Yaobang and Zhao Ziyang. Deng and the other elders overrode the Politburo in 1989 to impose Jiang Zemin as successor to the Party leadership.

Measured against these historical precedents, the current succession displays many firsts, all indicative of institutionalization:

- Jiang Zemin survived his full allotted time in office. He was installed as general secretary in 1989, and was reelected in 1992 and 1997, serving two-and-one-half terms (he assumed the Central Military Commission chairmanship in 1989 and the state presidency in 1992). His patron, Deng, did not remove him from office (although Deng considered doing so in 1992). Although Jiang was called to the top post in Beijing over the heads of Li Peng and Li Ruihuan, and had at times adversarial relations with both of them, neither tried to replace him. In consolidating his authority, Jiang engineered the fall from power of Yang Shangkun in 1992 and Qiao Shi in 1997, but neither of these men tried to unseat him.
- Jiang did not stay in office past the time when, according to the rules, he should have left office. In 1997, the Politburo established by consensus a new, informal rule that senior leaders should not be reappointed to another term after they reach the age of seventy. When this rule was established, Jiang was seventy-one, but he had himself declared a one-time exception to it, promising to retire in 2002. This promise, along with the fact that he would be seventy-six in 2002, were the main reasons why no serious consideration was given to his remaining in office, even though there was much speculation in the international press that he was trying to stay. The age seventy rule will also make it necessary for Jiang to retire from the post of Central Military Commission (CMC) chairman, a post for which there have never been either term or age limits, and to which the 1997 decision did not explicitly apply. Jiang's third post, the state presidency, is limited by the Constitution to two terms, which he has already served.
- Jiang Zemin was the first leader in the history of the People's Republic of China (PRC) not to select his own successor. Mao chose several successors

for himself (Liu Shaoqi, Lin Biao, and Hua Guofeng). So did Deng (Hu Yaobang, Zhao Ziyang, and Jiang Zemin). By contrast, Deng Xiaoping made Hu Jintao the PBSC's youngest member in 1992, and for the entire ten years of Hu's incumbency as informal successor-designate, Jiang Zemin did not challenge Hu's position. The incoming premier, Wen Jiabao, was recommended by Zhu Rongji over Jiang's choices, Wu Bangguo and Li Changchun.

- The retired elders (consisting after 1997 of Wan Li, Qiao Shi, Song Ping, Liu Huaqing, and several others) did not attempt to intervene in the succession or, indeed, in any decision. The right of three earlier elders (Deng Xiaoping, Chen Yun, and Li Xiannian) to intervene had been established by a secret Politburo resolution in 1987 and was reinforced by Deng's chairmanship of the Central Military Commission. This right was exercised to decisive effect during the 1989 Tiananmen crisis.[5] In 1997, Deng Xiaoping, the last of the three elders, died. A new group of elders was created by the retirements of Qiao Shi and others from the PBSC. The 1987 Politburo resolution was not renewed for them, nor did any of them sit on the CMC. These new elders received intra-Party documents and occasionally expressed their views,[6] but they did not attend Politburo meetings or exercise any decision-making power.
- The military exercised no influence over the succession. Although some senior military officers spoke in favor of Jiang's staying on in the position of CMC chair, they were ignored. They expressed no views on any other issue relating to the transfer of power. The succession of uniformed officers within the CMC echoes that in the civilian hierarchy: Senior officers associated with Jiang Zemin and over the age of seventy—Fu Quanyou and Yu Yongbo—have retired, to be replaced by a younger generation of officers. Following a tradition set in place in 1997, no uniformed officer was elected to the PBSC; the military representatives in Party Center were seated in the Politburo.
- The selection of the new Politburo was made by consensus within the old Politburo. The process was, to be sure, dominated by the senior members, and each of them tried and succeeded in placing associates in the successor body. But these factional considerations were played out within limits imposed by the need for a leadership consensus. None of the top leaders—Jiang, Li Peng, or Zhu Rongji—was powerful enough to force a nominee on his colleagues against their wills.

Never before in PRC history has there been a succession whose arrangements were fixed this far in advance, remained so stable to the end, and whose results so unambiguously transferred power from one generation of leaders to another. It is not that factions no longer exist, but that their powers are now in a state of mutual balance and that they have all learned a thing or two from the PRC's history. Political factions today have neither the power nor, perhaps more importantly, the will to upset rules that have been painfully arrived at. The absence of anyone with supreme power to upset these rules helps make them self-reinforcing.

MERITOCRACY MODIFIES FACTIONALISM

Factional considerations played a role in the succession process. But they were constrained by a twenty-year process of meritocratic winnowing that limited the list of candidates who could be considered in the final jockeying for position. Certainly, except for the period of the Cultural Revolution (1966–1976), there have always been both meritocratic and factional elements in promotions within the Chinese party–state. But until now, even at the most meritocratic times, the major criteria for promotion at the top were the ability to shift with changing political lines and personal loyalty to the top leader—first Mao Zedong, then Deng Xiaoping. While those among the new leading group are ideologically alert and politically savvy, and have mostly allied themselves with one senior leader or another, they rose to the top predominantly because of administrative skill, technical knowledge, educational background, and Party, rather than personal loyalty.

The start of this process was Deng Xiaoping's 1980 instruction to senior Party leaders to undertake a "four-way transformation" (*sihua*) of the cadre corps by finding and promoting cadres around the age of forty who were "revolutionary, younger, more educated, and more technically specialized" (*geminghua, nianqinghua, zhishihua, zhuanyehua*). In this way, Hu Jintao was promoted several levels by the CCP first secretary of Gansu Province, where he was then working; Wu Bangguo was promoted to party secretary of Shanghai's science and technology commission; and Wen Jiabao became deputy head of the provincial geology bureau in Gansu. The story was more or less the same for each member of the new Politburo.

In 1983, the CCP's Organization Department created a list of the most promising cadres of the "four transformations" generation, which it turned to whenever it needed to recommend a younger cadre for a post carrying ministerial rank. Hu Jintao was selected from this list to become Party secretary of Guizhou, Wen Jiabao to become deputy head of the powerful Central Party Office, and so on. The same cadre rejuvenation policy led Deng to order that someone younger than fifty be appointed to the Fourteenth Politburo Standing Committee in 1992. That choice fell upon Hu Jintao, so that his current accession to the position of General Secretary marks the orderly working out of the same process set in motion twenty years earlier.

Five of the nine members of today's new PBSC were members or alternate members of the Central Committee in 1982. This indicates the deliberateness and regularity of the succession process. The need to select PBSC members from the relatively small pool of candidates who survived the twenty-year selection process constrained the way in which factionalism worked between 2000 and 2002. Jiang Zemin could make the case for Zeng Qinghong or Zeng Peiyan, Li Peng for Luo Gan, and Zhu Rongji for Wen Jiabao, only on the basis of each person's excellent performance over the course of two decades in technically and administratively challenging jobs, and not because of symbolic importance (for example, Mao's promotion of Chen Yonggui) or ideological correctness (Mao's promotion of the so-called Gang of Four).

A norm of staff neutrality has become accepted to some degree at high levels within the Party Center, the State Council, and the Central Military Commission, so that the careers of rising stars have been relatively unperturbed by factional turmoil at the top. When Zhao Ziyang was purged in 1989, a few of his associates were immediately purged, but most of them were gradually moved into secondary bureaucratic posts over the course of the next couple of years. Some even continued to advance in their careers. Wen Jiabao, for example, served eight consecutive years as director of the powerful Party Central Office under three different general secretaries (Hu Yaobang, Zhao Ziyang, and Jiang Zemin). In contrast to the old spoils-like practices in which a leader's purge led quickly to the rooting-out of his followers several levels down the political system, the new system limits the damage that factional strife does to the orderly careers of the rising generation of leaders.

The product of this less factionalized, more regularized process is a competent leadership group that has high morale; that is politically balanced in representing different factions in the Party; that lacks one or two dominant figures, and is thus structurally constrained to make decisions collectively; and that is probably as collegial as any political leadership can be, because all the members came to the top through the same process, which they all view as having been broadly fair.[7]

Whether this event sets the template for future successions remains uncertain, but the chances of that happening are increased insofar as the current succession entrenches—as it does—rules that have elite support (for example, the age seventy rule), historical depth (the rules governing the meritocratic promotion system), and structural reinforcement from the informal political structure of balanced factional power.

INSTITUTIONAL DIFFERENTIATION WITHIN THE REGIME

At the high point of political reform in 1987, Zhao Ziyang proposed the "separation of Party and government" and the "separation of Party and enterprise." With Zhao's fall from power in 1989, these ideas were abandoned. Yet in the intervening fourteen years, much of what he proposed has happened by evolution, as the separation of responsibilities and spheres of authority—which Max Weber saw as definitive characteristics of the modern state—has gradually increased. What belongs to a given agency to handle is usually handled by that agency not only without interference, but with a growing sense that interference would be illegitimate.

One group of specialists, located in the Party center, manages ideology, mobilization, and propaganda (in the outgoing regime, it included people like Jiang Zemin, Li Ruihuan, Hu Jintao, and Zeng Qinghong). Another group, located in the State Council, makes economic policy (including Premier Zhu Rongji, vice-premiers Wen Jiabao and Wu Bangguo, most State Council members, and most provincial governors and Party secretaries). Provincial-level governors and Party secretaries have an increasingly wide scope to set local policy in such areas as education, health, welfare, the environment, foreign investment, and economic development. Many large state enterprises have now been removed from state ownership or placed under joint state–private ownership. Enterprise-management decisions are made on predominantly economic rather than political bases. State Council members, provincial-level officials, and enterprise managers are selected increasingly for their policy-relevant expertise. And economic policy makers at all levels suffer less and less frequently from intervention by the ideology-and-mobilization specialists.

The NPC has become progressively more autonomous, initiating legislation and actively reviewing and altering the proposals for legislation presented to it.[8] The police and courts remain highly politicized, but in the case of the courts, at least, a norm of judicial independence has been declared (in the 1994 Judges' Law and elsewhere) and judges are applying it more often in economic and criminal cases that are not sensitive enough to draw interference from Party authorities.

The military is still a "Party army," but it has also become smaller, more technically competent, and more professional. The officers being promoted to the CMC in the current succession are, as a group, distinguished more for their professional accomplishments and less for their political loyalties than was the case with previous CMC cohorts.[9] Calls have come, apparently from the younger members of the officer corps, to make the army a nonpartisan national force without the obligation to defend a particular ruling party. And although the incoming leader, Hu Jintao, has rejected these calls, the fact that they were voiced at all is a sign of a growing professional ethos within military ranks.[10]

All Chinese media are owned (at least formally, and for the most part actually) by Party and state agencies. But the media have become more commercialized and therefore less politicized. A handful of important outlets remain under variously direct control by the Party's propaganda department—for instance, *People's Daily,* the New China News Agency, China Central Television, provincial-level Party newspapers, the army newspaper, and so on. But to some extent, these media—and even more so, other newspapers, magazines, and radio or television stations around the country—fight for market share by covering movie and pop stars, sports, and scandals. In the political domain, they often push the envelope of what the regime considers off-limits by investigating stories about local corruption and abuses of power.

To be sure, the Chinese regime is still a party-state, in which the Party penetrates all other institutions and makes policy for all realms of action. And it is still a centralized, unitary system in which power at lower levels derives from grants by the center. But neither the top leader nor the central Party organs interfere as much in the work of other agencies as was the case under Mao and (less so) Deng. Ideological considerations have only marginal, if any, influence on most policy decisions. And staff members are promoted increasingly on the basis of their professional expertise in a relevant area.

All of this is partly to say, as has often been said before, that the regime is pragmatic. But behind the attitude of pragmatism lie increased institutional complexity, autonomy, and coherence—attributes that according to Huntington's theory should equip the regime to adapt more successfully to the challenges it faces.

INPUT INSTITUTIONS AND POLITICAL LEGITIMACY

One of the puzzles of the post-Tiananmen period has been the regime's apparent ability to rehabilitate its legitimacy (defined as the public's belief that the regime is lawful and should be obeyed) from the low point of 1989, when vast, nationwide pro-democracy demonstrations revealed the disaffection of a large segment of the urban population.

General theories of authoritarian regimes, along with empirical impressions of the current situation in China, might lead one to expect that the regime would now be decidedly low on legitimacy. Although authoritarian regimes often enjoy high legitimacy when they come to power, that legitimacy usually deteriorates for want of democratic procedures to cultivate ongoing consent. In the case of contemporary China, the regime's ideology is bankrupt. The transition from a socialist to a quasi-market economy has created a great deal of social unrest. And the regime relies heavily on coercion to repress political and religious dissent.

Direct evidence about attitudes, however, shows the contrary. In a 1993 nationwide random-sample survey conducted by Tianjian Shi, 94.1 percent of respondents agreed or strongly agreed with the statement that, "We should trust and obey the government, for in the last analysis it serves our interests." A 2002 survey by Shi found high percentages of respondents who answered similarly regarding both the central and local governments.[11] There is much other evidence from both quantitative and qualitative studies to suggest that expressions of dissatisfaction, including widely reported worker and peasant demonstrations, are usually directed at lower-level authorities, while the regime as a whole continues to enjoy high levels of acceptance.

A number of explanations can be offered for this pattern. Among them:

- Most people's living standards have risen during two decades of economic growth.
- The Party has co-opted elites by offering Party membership to able persons from all walks of life and by granting the informal protection of property rights to private entrepreneurs. This new direction in Party policy has been given ideological grounding in Jiang Zemin's theory of the "Three Represents," which says that the Party should represent advanced productive forces, advanced culture, and the basic interests of all the Chinese working people—that is, that it should stand for the middle classes as much as or more than the workers and peasants.
- The Chinese display relatively high interpersonal trust, an attitude that precedes and fosters regime legitimacy.[12]
- The Chinese population favors stability and fears political disorder. By pointing to the example of post-Communist chaos in Russia, the CCP has persuaded most Chinese, including intellectuals—from whom criticism might be particularly expected—that political reform is dangerous to their welfare.[13]
- Thanks to the success of political repression, there is no organized alternative to the regime.
- Coercive repression—in 1989 and after—may itself have generated legitimacy by persuading the public that the regime's grip on power is unshakeable. Effective repression may generate only resigned obedience at first, but to maintain cognitive consonance, citizens who have no choice but to obey a regime may come to evaluate its performance and responsiveness (themselves components of legitimacy) relatively highly.[14] In seeking psychological coherence, citizens may convince themselves that

their acceptance of the regime is voluntary—precisely because of, not despite, the fact that they have no alternative.

All these explanations may have value. Here, though, I would like to develop another explanation, more directly related to this essay's theme of institutionalization: The regime has developed a series of input institutions (that is, institutions that people can use to apprise the state of their concerns) that allow Chinese to believe that they have some influence on policy decisions and personnel choices at the local level.

The most thorough account of these institutions is Tianjian Shi's *Political Participation in Beijing,* which, although researched before 1989, describes institutions that are still in place. According to Shi, Chinese participate at the local and work-unit levels in a variety of ways. These include voting, assisting candidates in local-level elections, and lobbying unit leaders. Participation is frequent, and activism is correlated with a sense of political efficacy (defined as an individual's belief that he or she is capable of having some effect on the political system). Shi's argument is supported by the work of Melanie Manion, who has shown that in localities with competitive village elections, leaders' policy positions are closer to those of their constituents than in villages with noncompetitive voting.[15]

In addition to the institutions discussed by Shi and Manion, there are at least four other sets of input institutions that may help to create regime legitimacy at the mass level:

- The Administrative Litigation Act of 1989 allows citizens to sue government agencies for alleged violations of government policy. According to Minxin Pei, the number of suits stood in 1999 at 98,600 (see also his contribution to this volume). The success rate (determined by court victories plus favorable settlements) has ranged from 27 percent to around 40 percent. In at least one province, government financial support is now offered through a legal aid program to enable poor citizens to take advantage of the program.[16]
- Party and government agencies maintain offices for citizen complaints— letters-and-visits departments *(xinfangju)*—which can be delivered in person or by letter. Little research has been done on this process, but the offices are common and their ability to deal with individual citizen complaints may be considerable.
- As people's congresses at all levels have grown more independent— along with people's political consultative conferences, United Front structures that meet at each level just prior to the meeting of the people's congress—they have become an increasingly important channel by which citizen complaints may be aired through representatives.

- As the mass media have become more independent and market-driven, so too have they increasingly positioned themselves as tribunes of the people, exposing complaints against wrongdoing by local-level officials.

These channels of demand and complaint making have two common features. One is that they encourage individual rather than group-based inputs, the latter of which are viewed as threatening by the regime. The other is that they focus complaints against specific local-level agencies or officials, diffusing possible aggression against the Chinese party–state generally. Accordingly, they enable citizens to pursue grievances without creating the potential to threaten the regime as a whole.

AN AUTHORITARIAN TRANSITION?

Despite the institutionalization of orderly succession processes, meritocratic promotions, bureaucratic differentiation, and channels of mass participation and appeal, the regime still faces massive challenges to its survival. This essay does not attempt to predict whether the regime will surmount them. What we can say on available evidence is that the regime is not supine, weak, or bereft of policy options. In contrast with the Soviet and Eastern European ruling groups in the late 1980s and early 1990s, the new Chinese leaders do not feel that they are at the end of history. The policy statement excerpts contained in their investigation reports show that these leaders think they can solve China's problems.[17] They intend to fight corruption; reform the state-owned enterprises; ameliorate the lot of the peasants; improve the environment; comply with World Trade Organization rules while using transitional privileges to ease China's entry into full compliance; suppress political opposition; meet the challenge of U.S. containment; and, above all, stay in power and direct China's modernization. The argument that democratization, freedom, and human rights would lead to a truer kind of stability—as convincing as it may be to the democrats of the world—holds no appeal for these men.

The theoretical implications of China's authoritarian resilience are complex. For the last half-century, scholars have debated whether totalitarian regimes can adapt to modernity. The implications of the Chinese case for this discussion are twofold. First, in order to adapt and survive, the regime has had to do many of the things predicted by Talcott Parsons and those who elaborated his theory: The regime has had to abandon utopian ideology and charismatic styles of leadership; empower a technocratic elite; introduce bureaucratic regularization, complexity, and specialization; and reduce control over private speech and action. Second, contrary to the Parsonian prediction, these adaptations have not led to regime change. In Richard Lowenthal's terms, the regime has moved "from utopia to development."[18] But the Party has been able to do all these things without triggering a transition to democracy.

Although such a transition might still lie somewhere in the future, the experience of the past two decades suggests that it is not inevitable. Under conditions that elsewhere have led to democratic transition, China has made a transition instead from totalitarianism to a classic authoritarian regime, and one that appears increasingly stable.

Of course, neither society-centered nor actor-centered theories of democratic transition predict any particular outcome to be inevitable in any particular time frame. The Chinese case may, accordingly, merely reinforce the lesson that the outcome depends on politicians and their will to power. Alternatively, it may end up reminding us that democratic transition can take a long time. But it may also suggest a more disturbing possibility: that authoritarianism is a viable regime form even under conditions of advanced modernization and integration with the global economy.

NOTES

This chapter originally appeared under the title "Authoritarian Resilience" in the January 2003 (vol. 14, no. 1) issue of *Journal of Democracy.*

1. As an example, see the multiauthor symposium on Chinese democracy in *Journal of Democracy* 9 (January 1998).

2. In other words, to adapt a concept from democratic consolidation theory, the CCP has once again made itself the only game in town and is in the process of carrying out a successful transfer of power.

3. Samuel P. Huntington, *Political Order in Changing Societies* (New Haven, Conn.: Yale University Press, 1968), 12–24.

4. The factual base for this discussion is contained in Andrew J. Nathan and Bruce Gilley, *China's New Rulers: The Secret Files* (New York: New York Review Books, 2002), and is summarized in two articles in the *New York Review of Books,* 26 September and 10 October 2002. These publications are in turn based on Hairen Zong, *Disidai (The Fourth Generation)* (Carle Place, N.Y.: Mirror Books, 2002). Hairen Zong's account of the new generation of Chinese leaders is based on material contained in internal investigation reports on candidates for the new Politburo compiled by the Chinese Communist Party's Organization Department.

5. *The Tiananmen Papers: The Chinese Leadership's Decision to Use Force Against Their Own People—In Their Own Words,* Zhang Liang, comp., Andrew J. Nathan and Perry Link, eds. (New York: Public Affairs Books, 2001), 102, n. 1, and passim.

6. Hairen Zong, *Zhu Rongji zai 1999* (Zhu Rongji in 1999) (Carle Place, N.Y.: Mingjing Chubanshe, 2001); English translation edited by Andrew J. Nathan in *Chinese Law and Government* (January–February and March–April 2002).

7. Like any meritocratic process, of course, this one had elements of contingency. Hu Jintao's career is a good example, in particular his 1992 selection from among four candidates as the representative of the Fourth Generation to join the PBSC.

8. Michael Dowdle, "The Constitutional Development and Operations of the National People's Congress," *Columbia Journal of Asian Law* 12 (spring 1997): 1–125.

9. *Disidai*, ch. 11.

10. *Disidai*, ch. 1.

11. The 1993 survey was conducted for the project on "Political Culture and Political Participation in Mainland China, Taiwan, and Hong Kong." The 2002 survey was conducted for the project on "East Asia Barometer: Comparative Survey of Democratization and Value Changes." Data courtesy of Tianjian Shi.

12. Ronald Inglehart, *Modernization and Postmodernization: Cultural, Economic, and Political Change in 43 Societies* (Princeton, N.J.: Princeton University Press, 1997), 173, n. 2. Also Tianjian Shi, "Cultural Impacts on Political Trust: A Comparison of Mainland China and Taiwan," *Comparative Politics* 33 (July 2001): 401–19.

13. Christopher Marsh, "Learning From Your Comrade's Mistakes: The Impact of the Soviet Past on China's Future," *Communist and Post-Communist Studies* 35 (September 2003).

14. On components of legitimacy, see M. Stephen Weatherford, "Measuring Political Legitimacy," *American Political Science Review* 86 (March 1992): 149–66. The relationship I am proposing between successful coercion and legitimacy is hypothetical; so far as I know it has not been empirically established.

15. Tianjian Shi, *Political Participation in Beijing* (Cambridge, Mass.: Harvard University Press, 1997); Melanie Manion, "The Electoral Connection in the Chinese Countryside," *American Political Science Review* 90 (December 1996): 736–48.

16. Minxin Pei, "Citizens v. Mandarins: Administrative Litigation in China," *China Quarterly* (December 1997): 832–62, and personal communication. On legal aid, see *Disidai,* ch. 7; the province is Guangdong.

17. See Andrew J. Nathan and Bruce Gilley, *New Rulers,* chs. 7, 8.

18. Talcott Parsons, *The Social System* (New York: Free Press, 1951), 525–35; Richard Lowenthal, "Development vs. Utopia in Communist Policy," in Chalmers Johnson, ed., *Change in Communist Systems* (Stanford, Calif.: Stanford University Press, 1970), 33–116.

3

China's Invisible Social Revolution and Sino–American Cultural Relations

Carol Lee Hamrin

There is a social revolution underway in China that rarely makes the news headlines, but will be the central factor in reshaping the China of the future. Americans are already helping to shape this social and cultural change in quiet ways that are also under the media radar. A deep understanding of the complex change at the grassroots level in China, especially the role of Chinese and international faith-based organizations, is worth much more policy attention, for it is an area rife with bilateral . friction over religious and other human rights. Understanding this area is essential for any realistic government policy and for any effective business or organizational strategy.

CHINA'S SOCIETY MAKES A COMEBACK

Perhaps the least known "side effect" of China's rapid economic growth is the wholesale transformation in social structure underway. In early 2002, the Chinese Academy of Social Sciences (CASS) published the first official study of China's ongoing shift from a homogenous rural society to a much more diverse urban society.[1] By 2020, China will be an urban society (more than 50 percent of the population living in cities) for the first time in its history. From 2000 to 2010, 300 million people will move to cities of all sizes—the greatest migration in world history; and China's emerging middle class (those with an annual net income of $3,000 or more) already numbers nearly 100 million people and is growing about 20 percent per year.

The CASS report, which documents such changes, was the result of a three-year research project by nearly 100 sociologists. The report provides a portrait of an "embryonic modern social structure" and classifies Chinese society into ten occupational strata (see table 3.1). The report was published in part to justify President Jiang Zemin's recommendation that the Chinese Communist Party (CCP) recruit from the most advanced social groups, including new entrepreneurs.[2] After a popular reception over several months, however, the report was banned from further circulation due to controversy. Workers and farmers—the traditional constituency of the CCP—were placed near the bottom of the social ladder, while the first four strata (state and social administrators, managers, private business owners and professional/technical personnel) were praised as "representatives of advanced productive forces." This ranking fueled speculation that the Party was abandoning the newly poor for the newly rich.

How the political elite manages its complex and fluid relations with all these social groups and how they address the rapidly growing inequalities of wealth and resources, and the social tensions incumbent therewith, is probably the most important challenge facing the new leadership now coming into power. In any case, the secret is out. Fifty years after the CCP nationalized the economy, destroyed all independent social groups and launched a series of experiments to create new state-dominated social organizations, the trend is being reversed.

China's economic reform program has aimed at improving economic efficiency and sustaining rapid economic growth in order to compete in the global economy. Competing globally has been the goal, and the logic behind that goal, that of "globalization," in turn is reshaping China. *Globalization* is a shorthand term for a historic process involving a new level of international

---

Table 3.1. Classification of Chinese Society into Ten Occupational Strata.

   1. state and social administrators, 2.1 percent
   2. (enterprise) managers, 1.5 percent
   3. private business owners ("entrepreneurs"), 0.6 percent
   4. professional and technical personnel, 5.1 percent
   5. office staff, 4.8 percent
   6. self-employed business people, 4.2 percent (admittedly a low estimate)
   7. commercial and service staff, 12 percent
   8. industrial workers, 22.6 percent
   9. agricultural workers, "the largest" percentage, but declining
  10. the unemployed and semi-employed, 3.1 percent and expanding

Source: Lu Xueyi, ed., *Dangdai zhongguo shehui jiecheng yanjiu baogao* [*Research Report on Social Strata in Contemporary China*] (Beijing: Shehui kexue wenxian chubanshe, 2002).

integration—the acknowledgement of international norms, the spread of new technologies, especially in communication, and an unprecedented rate of change. The logic of globalization is individual choice among competing alternatives in the market of goods and services, lifestyles and loyalties. The extension of the global economic market thus gives birth to social, cultural and eventually political pluralism.

CHINA JOINS THE GLOBAL "ASSOCIATIONAL REVOLUTION"

Reflecting a global trend to downsize government and free up economies, China has set a goal of creating a "small state, large society." To lighten the heavy load of central state subsidies for social services, this responsibility was given to local governments. They, in turn, have sought help from the non-state sector in "burden sharing." Nonprofit organizations (NPOs) have been set up as arms of the state but have also sprung up spontaneously at the grass-roots level.

Along with a more open and pluralistic society and the rising middle class has come a proliferation of public institutions, which number well over 200,000.[3] These range from membership-based "social organizations" to private charities and foundations. There are consumer groups as well as chambers of commerce, and advocacy organizations such as environmental and women's legal aid groups. Few of these nonprofits are truly nongovernmental organizations (NGOs), since the state still exercises strong influence over structure, personnel and finances, but the trend is toward greater autonomy. Pioneer "GONGOS" (a tongue-in-check oxymoron for China's "government-organized NGOs") were set up by state agencies primarily as affiliates to raise foreign funds, which usually are matched by in-kind domestic contributions (labor, land, construction, and the like).

The competitive pressure from the grass-roots organizations, especially in the area of humanitarian social services, has forced even China's top-down NPOs to allow foreign participation as well as funding, to develop a domestic donor base and, increasingly, to promote the interests of their constituencies, and not just state goals.

Leading State-Organized Institutions (SOIs)

- The China Association of NGOs (CANGOS) was founded in 1991 as an umbrella organization for the nonprofit sector. Its creation was a first step toward separating nonprofit activity from government departments.

- The China Youth Development Foundation (founded in 1985 by the Communist Youth League) and its leading charity, Project Hope, pioneered domestic fundraising for poor students nationwide. For example, in Xinjiang they helped 40,000 school dropouts return to school and built seventy-six primary schools and 252 school libraries from 1990–1999.[4]
- The China Charities Federation (CCF), since 1994 the official "umbrella" organization for relief aid and social welfare, is an arm of the Ministry of Civil Affairs (MCA). Under the leadership of former MCA executive vice president Yan Mingfu, CCF has improved accountability and international recognition for China's Third Sector as a whole.
- Since the early 1980s, the Amity Foundation has been a channel for outside funding and services from Protestant religious organizations. Amity is affiliated with the China Christian Council and registered under the Party's United Front Department. At first, Amity focused on English teaching and on eastern China, but it now also has departments for rural development, social welfare, medical and health work focused on southwest China. Amity is respected by others in China's Third Sector for the quality of its work. The official Catholic church in China also has its counterpart affiliates, and the Beifang Jinde Social Service Center was set up in 1998 in Shijiazhuang, Hebei Province.[5]

Other Faith-Based Chinese NGOs

Small-scale local social service agencies are linked directly to local congregations or religious associations. One interesting example is the Signpost Youth Club affiliated with Ningbo's Catholic diocese in Zhejiang Province. A "virtual" club, it uses the Internet to promote spiritual formation for younger Catholics (ages eighteen to thirty) working and studying in different parts of the province.[6]

Another example of a registered but independent faith-based organization is the Holy Love Foundation in Chengdu. A young couple, taking pity on idle handicapped youth unable to attend school, registered the foundation in 1992 under a business sponsor. They raised funds to refurbish an old warehouse into a boarding school. Board members include a government representative from the bureau of civil affairs, which takes up to 1 percent of donations. The school has survived several crises with bureaucrats and developers due to the influence of grateful parents and local popularity from winning Special Olympics events.[7]

The YMCA/YWCA in China, headquartered in Shanghai with branches in ten cities, is a state-run NPO with a long pre-1949 history. The Shanghai branch is pioneering a new type of multi-functional community center to provide better services than those available from the government street offices.[8]

Charitable efforts by unregistered religious groups often are spontaneous responses to pressing needs out of good conscience. One elderly woman, for example, took in abandoned babies but her unregistered Protestant house church has had difficulty buying property or getting permits for an orphanage. Senior leaders of a large partnership of Protestant house church networks that met in early 2002 listed such "social ministries" among six top priorities for the Chinese church, and invited foreign cooperation.[9]

THE INTERNATIONAL FACTOR

International NGOs (INGOs) have made major contributions to China's economic and social development. Authors of the *Directory of International NGOs Supporting Work in China*[10] concluded that China was receiving well over $100 million each year in project funding directly from or channeled through over 500 INGOs and foundations. Gifts in kind, such as hundreds of thousands of volumes of books, would add substantially to that total. As of 2000, there were at least seventy grant-making foundations, seventy advocacy groups, 200 humanitarian organizations, and 150 faith-based charitable groups, all foreign-based, involved in China (the latter figure included 100 organizations working through Amity Foundation and is therefore a low estimate).

Pioneers in U.S.–China elite-level cultural relations include the Committee on Scholarly Communication with China and the National Committee on U.S.–China Relations. Beginning with exchanges involving cultural, media and political–legal elites, they are now exploring new territory such as privatization of education. This is in addition to the many educational ties that have been established between colleges and universities, including Christian colleges and seminaries.

Other major actors include the Ford and Asia Foundations, which have offices in Beijing and budgets ranging from $4 million to $9 million annually. These and other INGOs began in the 1980s to support educational and professional development and exchanges, reviving the social sciences in China, and then branched out in the 1990s to support projects in civil society, law, and governance. The Asia foundation sponsors monthly forums and a networking website (www.ChinaNPO.net) for the China NPO Network.

FAITH-BASED CONTRIBUTIONS

The Third Sector has also become home to many international faith-based organizations, many of whom renewed earlier mission-era ties to China and now often work in the poor interior and at the grassroots county level in China. The ecumenical United Board for Christian Higher Education in Asia is an example. The United Board has focused on enhancing education for women and ethnic minorities in more isolated tertiary institutions. Most church-based or denominational organizations, including China service organizations of the Mennonites and the Maryknoll Brothers, work in partnership with official faith-based counterparts. Most "parachurch" and many mission agencies find partners in their special functional sector or "niche." For example, thousands of teachers of English or professional skills have been sent by organizations working jointly with the Foreign Experts Bureau and state educational organs. One international institute with expertise in linguistics affiliates with state institutions responsible for minority nationalities. At several grassroots locations, they help sponsor dual language schools.

The Jianhua Foundation, CEDAR Fund, and Caritas have been pioneers among the many humanitarian INGOs that work out of Hong Kong. Along with the Beijing division of the Christian Broadcasting Network (CBN–China, www.cbnchina.org), these groups do humanitarian work at all levels through China's charity federations or Red Cross and the government bureaus responsible for the specific types of projects.

WESTERN DEVELOPMENT

Many humanitarian INGOs got their start providing relief to areas in China struck by disaster in the late 1990s. The Salvation Army and World Vision International (see www.wvi.org), along with Oxfam, are the largest INGOs involved in relief and antipoverty work. Responding to the government's encouraging of international participation in antipoverty and development work in west China and home to most of China's poor ethnic minorities, these groups have expanded support for microloan projects and holistic community development projects.

Some localized efforts have been developed by expatriates responding to warm welcomes in areas where grandparents or parents had served as missionaries. Examples include the Evergreen Family Friendship Services in Shanxi Province and Gansu Inc., a U.S. nonprofit that brings ophthalmologists to teach and perform cataract surgery for poor villagers, choosing a different county hospital base each summer.[11]

REGULATORY PROBLEMS AND CORRUPTION

Bureaucratic red tape and corruption, which are now covered more extensively in the media, are still major hindrances to healthy social development. All nonstate social organizations are heavily regulated and closely monitored. The red tape gives headaches and teaches patience to all who seek to operate within official boundaries. Specific regulations and style of implementation vary somewhat by sector and locality, but tend to share the following characteristics:

- There is a dual control system: government registration and functional affiliation. Oversight of most nonprofits is carried out by the Ministry of Civil Affairs, but there are specialized agencies for labor, youth, religious and women's groups.
- Day-to-day line supervision is carried out by functional Party or government agencies or their designated monopolies. Their supervision is comprehensive and includes oversight of the application for and the approval of registration, the political and ideological work done through Party branches, finance and accounting, personnel management, policy research, and external relations.
- Before registration, organizations must meet strict standards, such as a designated work place, certified professional staff, a minimum number of members, proof that no other similar local organization already exists, and that there is a "need" for the service. Some of these prerequisites such as renting, hiring, and recruiting that must occur *before registration* are technically illegal until *after registration.*

Accountability in the Third Sector is a major issue that must be addressed soon for the sector to gain public and foreign confidence. Fundraising so far has focused on outside donors; a typical Chinese NPO is funded 80 percent from overseas and 20 percent from Hong Kong. Fundraising inside China is still quite new and for the most part restricted to national GONGOs. While the 1999 law on donations allows individuals and corporations to donate money, it is not clear about the right to solicit funds, including through the state-controlled media. Tax benefits for giving are even more recent.

Like many laws and regulations in China, the requirements for NPOs are so vague, contradictory, or burdensome that they end up being circumvented or ignored. Consequently there is a large gray area of semiautonomy and semilegality in which nonprofits "push the envelope" of bureaucratic controls in order to get things done. To gain more freedom, organizations doing nonprofit work often register as businesses or register through personal relationships involving little restriction. This can lead to either creativity or corruption![12]

NPOs closely tied to the government are often misused by bureaucratic supervisors scavenging for funds. Many local charity federations have a bad reputation, and the YMCA was notorious for corruption and abuse of power under the former director and his family. A huge controversy in 2002 over alleged illegality in Project Hope's fundraising efforts has forced more public attention onto the mechanisms of accountability in the Third Sector as a whole. Its sponsors at the Youth Development Foundation have requested a formal government audit to prove their innocence.[13] Accountability is a special challenge for unregistered grassroots humanitarian efforts, given the inexperience with management and auditing and the temptations of handling cash or funding through personal accounts. One now successful suburban "halfway house" ministry to "street boys" and handicapped orphans, for example, suffered an early crisis due to the founding director's embezzling funds from overseas Chinese Christian supporters.[14]

As a result of all these problems, the Chinese public remains leery of giving. The chronic "catch-22" situations for Chinese NGOs also affect their partnering INGOs and foundations. There is also a sad history of harassment of prominent INGOs, in the guise of re-registration or inspection, due to suspicion of their potential role as Trojan horses for Western values. It is not accidental that regulations for INGO operation in China have been delayed time and again. They have been promised by "the end of the year" every year since 1999!

NGOS—A "HOT TOPIC"

The study of the nonprofit sector has become an intellectual "fever" in China. Tsinghua University has set up China's first Center for the Study of NGOs as part of its School of Public Policy and Management. The Center sponsored China's first conference on NPOs in October 1999, with the support of the Asia Foundation, and other specialized conferences have followed. The China NPO Network has registered as an enterprise with the Bureau of Industry and Commerce in order to become a for-profit provider of training and information services for the Third Sector. The Network has an initiative underway to create an accreditation mechanism and training curriculum in partnership with the faith-based Maclellan Foundation of Chattanooga, Tennessee.

The Chinese have actively joined the international discussion of the worldwide growth of associational activity. An example at the elite level is the popularity of the lectures and writings by the acknowledged global "guru" of nonprofit studies, Professor Lester Salamon, Director of the Center for Civil Society Studies at Johns Hopkins University. Both domestic and foreign businesses are showing new interest in philanthropy, and the U.S.–China Business Council helps introduce such opportunities to its members. Creative use of popular media for NPO outreach is beginning to shape public awareness as well. Shanghai TV and the Shanghai Charity Federation in 1999 cosponsored the first weekly television entertainment show, "The Love Program," which was hosted by sports stars and promoted charity by showing one poor family receiving aid during each program.[15]

Further developments occurred in June 2002, when the State Office for Public Sector Reform launched the third phase of a joint program which began in 1990 with the United Nations Development Program and China's International Center for Economic and Technical Exchanges. Their next five-year reform effort will redefine nonprofit and public institutions to clarify and strengthen their autonomy and encourage a stronger market role.[16] Policies are also being introduced to lift limits on total NPO investment and offer tax breaks or exemptions as well as favorable treatment regarding customs, foreign exchange, and land use rights.

This new thinking about the importance of nongovernmental, nonprofit activities is helping to fuel positive cultural change. There is a growing sense of "citizenship," whereby the state is to serve the interests of its citizens, not the people serving interests defined solely by the state. Individuals see themselves as creators of their own multiple loyalties and identities, able to choose to "consume" the state's socialist or nationalist ideology and agenda—or not. There is also a growing "rights awareness" and resort to lobbying or litigation to improve the rule of law for social organizations.

These trends will accelerate as the government carries out plans to further privatize social service institutions as well as expand the role of nonprofits. This will expand opportunities to establish nonprofit schools and hospitals, all of which until recently were solely state-owned. As the 1990s witnessed the de facto privatization of thousands of state-owned enterprises (SOEs) through bankruptcy, the coming decade will witness the privatization of thousands of SOIs (state-owned institutions), which are morally bankrupt.

POLICY CHANGES LIKELY UNDER CHINA'S NEW LEADERSHIP

The rapid social and cultural changes will force China's new leadership to revise the current reactionary social and religious policies. Since 1999, the leadership has tried to reassert state control mechanisms over society in an attempt to assure stability during the leadership succession and the initial implementation of WTO-related economic restructuring, including the massive layoffs of state employees. The results have included a spike in religious persecution and other human rights abuses, with tighter regulations and state intrusion into the management of official social and religious organizations and efforts to shut down all those not registered. The repression has produced a buildup of social grievances, incipient anti-government social movements, such as the Falun Gong, as well as widespread elite expectations for renewed social and political reforms, all of which will escalate into demands on new leaders.

Preparation of the Sixteenth Party Congress platform, which set forth goals for the next five years, spurred a search behind the scenes for alternative means of governing society. For example, Lu Xueyi, director of the CASS report research group, argued for new social policies to promote social justice. He pointed out that expanded gaps in income distribution are due to the spontaneous nature of social change to date, in which social policies have not played due regulatory roles. "The innovation of social systems seriously lags behind," Lu asserted, "hampering the relatively free movement among different strata. The residence registration system, in particular, puts the vast majority of farmers in structural inequality." In accordance with the principle of social justice, Lu stressed that "spontaneous development of the structure of social strata will not work. The State must play a guiding role . . . in [new] system arrangements and policy options."[17]

The Sixteenth Party Congress internal policy review has given us glimpses of new options that may surface in the next few years. To keep alive the option of gradual peaceful change, new leaders may begin to move beyond the Deng Jiang program sooner rather than later. International trends also will continue to drive change as China seeks to compete globally. The following is a portrait of the logic behind future change.

SOCIAL REFORMS TO BUILD SOCIAL CAPITAL

Chinese society is not only experiencing a confusion of competing value systems, but a severe moral and spiritual crisis that endangers sustained progress.[18] The dominant public values are suspicion and factionalism from the communist "power struggle culture," combined with the greed of the 1990s market boom, which leaves China with the worst of both socialism and capitalism—rule of the lawless. Endemic cheating in the education system and fraud in consumer products and services, as well as media revelations of major official corruption scandals, all have prompted heated public debate on the Internet about the lack of integrity and honesty.[19]

Academics and policy think tanks have begun to focus on this notable lack of public virtues and habits that foster trust and cooperation, and have begun to explore development theories suggesting that this "social capital" is as important as financial capital for a healthy market economy. A Party document that launched an "ethics-building campaign" in 2001 spoke optimistically of combining values from Chinese tradition, the revolutionary tradition, and modern international experience. Francis Fukuyama, however, argues that such top-down government intervention to create social capital distorts the results in ways that actually inhibit economic development. In particular, state-fostered Chinese nationalism works against the growing cosmopolitanism that complements globalization. Genuinely shared public morality and social creativity requires freedom of association to promote truly voluntary community cooperation so that people can experience self-direction and learn new civic concepts and skills.[20]

GOVERNMENT POWER-SHARING

Chinese are fully aware that governments everywhere are cutting back the welfare state. As part of this trend, the World Bank is seeking to empower Chinese community organizations in their development projects. NGO pioneers are learning from the vibrant nonprofit sectors in Hong Kong, Taiwan, and Singapore. At an international conference on poverty reeducation in Beijing in October 2001, NGO organizers offered to act as the "vanguard" in cooperation with international counterparts, as well as with Chinese government and business, in exploring new models for poverty alleviation.[21]

To address the tidal wave of social change coming over the next ten years, pioneers in the various elites are beginning to undergo a fundamental paradigm shift. Influential policy researchers have developed a rationale for moving beyond state corporatism to societal corporatism, with increasing autonomy for nonprofits and grassroots initiatives.[22] There is talk of win-win-win alliances among government, business, and social organizations to create a new three-sector governance model. The "reinvention of governance" is already under discussion. Shanghai's mayor, for example, has stressed the need to change the functions of the government. Shenzhen's vice

mayor has spoken of replacing the command-type government with a ser-
vice-oriented government within three to five years.[23]

"GREATER CHINA"
INTEGRATION IN NONECONOMIC AREAS

China's future lies in stronger ties with global Chinese networks based in the
United States, Hong Kong, Taiwan, and Singapore. These societies, which
have made the best economic showings in Asia, are based on U.S.–U.K.
common law norms and institutions rather than on "statist" European socialist systems that more closely fit the continental civil law system enshrined in China's constitution. Taiwan's democratization and the looming
2007 date for direct elections in Hong Kong provide a pragmatic rationale
for mainland reforms that might close the institutional gap in noneconomic
arenas and thus keep open the possibility of future unification through convergence of systems.

The same logic comes from the need to reverse China's brain drain. Employing the highly educated in all sectors has become a top priority for
Chinese leaders as they seek to create a "knowledge economy" to keep
from falling behind global frontrunners. Coastal city governments adver-
tise for foreign experts (of which there were 220,000 in China in 2000),
and educated Chinese overseas are beginning to return at a higher rate. But
given a global shortage of top professionals, top quality Chinese will come
back to live in China in significant numbers only when they are convinced
their rights, including those of belief and association, will be respected and
protected.

ACCOMMODATION OF CULTURAL PLURALISM

To foster nonviolent cultural competition the state will need to give up its totalistic aspirations and its myopic negative view of the role of religion in society and will need to share moral and social authority. One high level official recently called for a total revamping of Leninist theories on religion, to
accommodate the new mix of values and religions that is today's reality. Soci-
ologist Peter Berger's research on cultural globalization has identified the four
most dynamic global cultures—elite business culture, its twin of popular consumer culture, academic culture with its focus on science and individual rights,
and evangelical/charismatic Protestant culture[24]—all of which are quite evident
in China and share the singular characteristic of globalization, that of individ-

ual choice in a pluralistic environment. The most modernized Chinese—urban professionals living in southern California—are changing the definition of what it means to be modern and Chinese, being 30 to 40 percent Christian in their identity and lifestyle. It is important to note that all four of these global cultures have been conditioned by their transmission through global Chinese networks. Pop culture has even been termed *Tai-Gang* (Taiwan-Hong Kong) culture.

Add to this mix the growing number of New Religious Movements (NRMs), both from the outside and from new combinations of elements of indigenous traditional culture, including elite Confucianism as well as popular folk religion, and it is evident that China's religious policy is hopelessly out of date. Even at the local level in remote areas of China, there is now a complex mix of partially competing, partially cooperating cultural leaders.

IMPLICATIONS FOR A REALISTIC U.S. HUMAN RIGHTS POLICY

As new Chinese leaders begin to address these daunting social challenges, the most obvious implication for U.S. policy makers is to pay attention—not just to politics and economics at the elite level, but to the complex changes underway in grassroots society. China's social problems are the Achilles' heel of the regime and the nation, and their ability to handle these problems is of tremendous importance both to the United States and the global economy and security. Beijing is increasingly focused on its internal security problems, which further complicates its options in relating to the outside world. And all decision makers planning for interchange with China need to listen to Americans involved on the ground. This factor was missing, for example, in the highly unrealistic debate over the Most Favored Nation–Permanent Normal Trade Relations (MFN–PNTR) status for China a few years back. Recommendations for trade sanctions in response to Chinese human rights abuses came mainly from human rights NGOs and religious lobbyists who lacked experience in China, while counter suggestions from nonpolitical NGOs based in China more in tune with Chinese popular views were ignored. For example, during a China trip in late 1997, this author took an informal poll of the opinions of more than thirty Chinese Christians along the whole spectrum of relations with the state and found unanimous and strongly felt support for MFN–PNTR status to keep China's door open to resources of all kinds that gave them more autonomy from the state. Yet the policy disagreement was depicted falsely instead as a clash between moralists who cared about human rights and greedy businesses which cared only for profits.

Other policy implications include the following:

- Improvements in human rights will not come overnight from the top down, but will come gradually through grassroots cultural change and social activism as people begin to defend their own interests. Future Chinese governments at all levels need ideas and assistance to deal creatively with social problems. There will be room for mutual cooperation that directly or indirectly protects human rights. For example, the bilateral rule of law initiative should encompass laws affecting religious practice. There could also be a labor management initiative as part of discussions on WTO.
- Chinese policy is more likely to change when it can be perceived as voluntary participation in regional international human rights activities rather than as a forced response to bilateral pressure. Thus, U.S. government initiatives should be "internationalized" or "Asianized" whenever possible.
- In order to be effective, outside actors need to think beyond "China" as a single national entity and begin to deal creatively with the reality of varied local situations and the needs of local governments. For example, human rights monitors could report on differences in local conditions, using a praise and blame approach to fuel competition among local governments to improve their relative reputation and risk rating among investors, both businesses and nonprofits.
- In promoting social and cultural change in China, the role of the U.S. federal government or national commissions, as well as international organizations, is limited. State and city governments—in cooperation with their business, religious, and civic organizations—may play an increasing role as authority in China shifts to the provincial level. Private sector and nongovernmental organizations will be the main outside agents of change.
- Expectations need revising. The outcome of near-term change will most likely not be the U.S. model of limited government and federalism. Chinese culture still grants the state supreme authority in society and both the historical experience and the legal structure are closer to a continental European model.

In sum, a U.S. human rights policy composed of sticks without carrots hurts important, albeit unrecognized, interests. Korea and Taiwan are prime examples of how the United States can help build more open and democratic societies in Asia. If we want people to change, we have to help them change.

NOTES

1. Xueyi Lu, ed., *Dangdai Zhongguo Shehui Jiecheng Yanjiu Baogao* (*Research Report on Social Strata in Contemporary China*), Shehui Kexue Wenxian Chubanshe (Beijing: Social Sciences Documentation Publishers), 2002.

2. See Jiang Zemin, Speech at the meeting celebrating the eightieth anniversary of the CCP, July 1, 2001, *Beijing Review* (19 July 2001).

3. Josephine Ma, "Sect Fears Put New NGO Laws on Hold," *South China Morning Post,* 15 October 2001.

4. *Xinhua English News*, 8 December 1999.

5. Author's interviews with Amity staff in Nanjing and other NGO staff in Beijing and Shanghai, June 2001. See <www.amityfoundation.org> (14 April 2003), and information from the *China Church Quarterly* newsletter (spring 2002). See <www.chinacatholic.org/bfjinde> (14 April 2003).

6. "Young Catholics Explore Internet to Maintain Faith," *UCAN News Service.*

7. Personal conversations with the directors in Chengdu, 1997, and communication with supporters in the United States, 2002.

8. Author's interview with the director of the Asia Foundation office in Beijing, June 2001. The Luoshan Citizen Services Center now provides nursing care, daycare, and a gym; its hotline helps callers with complaints link with appropriate government agencies for redress.

9. David Wang, "What House Church Leaders Discussed," *Asian Report* 249 (January/February 2002).

10. China Development Research Services, 1999.

11. Author's interviews in Gansu, November 1997, and in Taiyuan and Yangqu, Shanxi, November 1997 and 2000.

12. Tony Saich, "Negotiating the State: The Development of Social Organizations in China," *China Quarterly* 161 (March 2000): 124–141.

13. Personal communication with a Project Hope leader, March–April 2002.

14. Personal communication with a supporter, June 2002.

15. *Xinhua English News*, 13 February 1999. More recently, according to Knight Ridder, 6 June 2002, a young former stockbroker set up a private charity hotline in 2000. The publicity generated a flood of calls. After his personal savings ran out, the program was scaled back but continues.

16. *People's Daily*, 19 June 2002, <http://www.china.org.cn/english/2002/Jun/34976.htm> (19 June 2002).

17. Cited in Pipi Lu, "Ten Strata of Chinese Society," *Beijing Review* 45, no. 12 (2002).

18. Jinghao Zhou, *Remaking China's Public Philosophy for the Twenty-First Century* (Westport, Conn.: Praeger, 2003).

19. Bruce Gilley, "People's Republic of Cheats," *Far Eastern Economic Review* (21 June 2001): 59–60.

20. See Francis Fukuyama, "Social Capital and Civil Society." Paper presented at the IMF Conference on Second Generation Reforms, 1 October 1999,

<www.imf.org/external/pubs/ft/seminar/1999/reforms/fukuyama.htm> (14 April 2003). This "second wave of reforms" is to produce the social and cultural development necessary for sustaining economic development.

21. Conference Report, *Xinhuanet*, 30 October 2001.

22. Xiaoguang Kang, "China's Social Organizations in Transition," <www.chinanpo.org> (25 June 2001).

23. Quoted in "China's WTO Membership—Now the Hard Part Begins," Willy Wo-Lap Lam, *CNN Online*, 13 November 2001.

24. Peter Berger, "Four Faces of Global Culture," *The National Interest* (fall 1997): 23–29.

4

Domestic Changes in China and Implications for American Policy

Minxin Pei

One of the most important strategic goals in the United States' policy toward China is the eventual transformation of the Chinese political system. During the Cold War, the overwhelming priority given to the containment of the Soviet Union overrode the desire for the promotion of democracy and human rights in China, which at that time was ruled by one of the most repressive regimes in its history. Since the end of the Cold War, however, debate on Washington's China policy has revolved around the issue of the benefits of a policy of engagement in general, and the question of whether such a policy would eventually encourage the emergence of democratic political institutions in the world's largest authoritarian regime.[1] During the Clinton administration, engagement with China was often justified by invoking the liberal theory that linked economic development with democratization, even though President Bill Clinton's reversal on tying China's Most Favored Nation (MFN) trade status to its human rights improvement had severely undercut the credibility of his policy. The liberal rationale was also applied to the argument for bringing China into the World Trade Organization (WTO) toward the end of the Clinton era, despite few ostensible signs that the Chinese leadership would be willing to relinquish the Chinese Communist Party's (CCP) political supremacy as a result of economic development.

Even the advent of a Republican administration under George W. Bush has not put an end to the hope that economic development will bring political change in China. Despite the early talk of "strategic competition" with China and the adoption of a much more hard-line approach to Beijing, a Bush administration infused with geopolitical realism has also identified the emergence of democracy in China as a key strategic goal. In President Bush's new

National Security Strategy he declared, "America will encourage the advancement of democracy and economic openness in [Russia and China], because these are the best foundations for domestic stability and international order."[2] While few would dispute the strategic benefits of a democratic transformation of China's political system, many may doubt the short-term prospects of such a proposition, especially given the relatively few policy instruments the United States has in directly effecting democratic changes in one of the world's major powers that guards its own sovereignty as jealously as does the United States.

Short-term skepticism about the feasibility of China's democratic transformation, however, should not be accepted as grounds for abandoning a worthy strategic objective. In fact, a comprehensive examination of U.S. engagement with China since the historic Nixon trip yields a more encouraging assessment: even though China has not undergone a complete democratic transformation that would have fundamentally altered U.S.–China relations, American engagement with China over the last thirty years—especially since the restoration of diplomatic relations in 1979—has created an international environment extremely conducive to China's undertaking of domestic reforms. These reforms have gradually transformed Chinese society, economy and, to a lesser extent, politics. The overall trends over the last thirty years—China's full integration into the international community, rapid economic modernization, and significant expansion of personal freedoms and tentative steps taken toward political reform (as discussed in the previous chapters)—reflect positively on the U.S. policy of engagement. Indeed, the Bush Administration has noted these progressive developments. In the President's National Security Strategy, China is described as having "begun to take the road to political openness, permitting many personal freedoms and conducting village-level elections."[3]

The challenge for the United States is thus how to become a force of influence in the social and political evolution of China. In the past quarter-century, the United States contributed to China's economic reform and gradual political openness by creating a set of structural incentives for Beijing's leaders to adopt such policies (the two most important incentives include access to American markets, technology, and capital, and a nonconfrontational strategic posture in East Asia). In the future, domestic social and political changes in China will require the United States to fine-tune its approach so that it can leverage its influence more effectively in promoting political opening in China. Such an adjustment, in tactics rather than in strategy, is urgently needed because China may be entering a period in which the growing incongruence between its relatively closed political system and its fast-changing society is raising doubts about both the sustainability of the Chinese reform model and the complacency about the current U.S. policy toward China.

This chapter is divided into four parts. The first part describes social changes in China since the late 1970s, while the second analyzes changes in Chinese political institutions. The third part then examines two pathologies caused by the disparities between China's political system and its fast-changing economy and society, while the last section probes policy implications for the United States.

SOCIAL CHANGE IN CHINA SINCE 1979

Since China embarked on its historic journey of economic reform and modernization in the late 1970s, Chinese society has undergone unprecedented changes in terms of structure, autonomy, and values. The primary driving force for social change is economic development and reform. As income levels continue to rise, China's social structure has become more diverse and plural. In addition, the massive migration from the rural sector into modern sectors, coupled with the emergence of new industries and the growth of various professions, have dramatically increased social mobility. These changes have given Chinese society greater autonomy while gradually undercutting the state's control over society.

ECONOMIC AUTONOMY

Economic autonomy is the most important source of a society's independence from state control. Conceptually, economic autonomy may be understood as the amount of resources controlled by nonstate actors in a society. A simple measure of the degree of a society's economic autonomy is the private sector's share of the GDP. Judged by this measure, the level of economic autonomy of Chinese society has risen significantly since 1979. For example, in 1978, state-owned enterprises (SOEs) produced about 78 percent of China's total industrial output, while collectively-owned firms contributed the rest (there were no foreign-owned firms). But in 1999, the share of industrial output contributed by SOEs plummeted to 28 percent while collectively-owned firms and foreign-owned enterprises accounted for, respectively, 39 and 33 percent of industrial output.[4]

The rising economic autonomy of Chinese society is also reflected in employment data. The number of jobs in SOEs continued to decline in relative terms, while employment opportunities in the nonstate sector grew explosively. In 1978, for example, employment in SOEs accounted for 60 percent of nonagricultural jobs; but in 1999, the share of employment in SOEs fell to about 30 percent—half of its level twenty years earlier.[5] Declining state control over the economy has allowed average Chinese citizens unprecedented freedom in employment, residence, and consumer choices. In theory, this trend should, over time, help foster a more open society because a citizenry less economically dependent on the state will be more able to assert its rights and autonomy. Another important effect of the growth of the private sector is the diversion of elites from politics into commerce.

Increasingly, the attractiveness of the private sector enticed a large number of government officials to "jump into the sea" (the Chinese phrase for becoming private entrepreneurs). However, this trend can cut both ways. On the one hand, the infusion of talents previously employed by the state should enhance the stock of human capital in the private sector. Presumably, the loss of the same talents should also weaken the state. But in a mixed economy with a high degree of state control, the exodus of officials into the private sector can also facilitate the growth of crony capitalism and corruption. In the Chinese case, much evidence suggests that the risks of crony capitalism have grown significantly as a result of the marriage between a politically weak private sector and a state extensively involved in economic activities.

SOCIAL PLURALISM

Economic modernization is also a powerful force for social pluralism in China. In recent years, economic growth has spurred the emergence of new service professions, such as accounting, law, information management, financial services, and real estate. The rising level of specialization in the economy increases social diversity and indirectly enhances the power of markets over the state (mainly because a society with a higher level of specialization allows individuals greater choices). Social diversification is politically significant because this process creates professionals, a key component of a middle class. Indeed, Chinese social indicators suggest that increasing specialization has led to the rapid emergence of the core elements of a middle class. (See table 4.1.)

Table 4.1. Growth of Managerial and Professional Groups in China (as a percentage of the population).

	1952	1978	1999
Managers	0.14	0.23	1.5
Professionals	0.86	3.48	5.1
White collar workers	0.5	1.29	4.8
Total	1.5	5.0	11.4

Source: Lu Xueyi, ed., *Dangdai zhongguo shehui jiecheng yanjiu baogao* [*Research Report on Social Strata in Contemporary China*] (Beijing: Shehui kexue wenxian chubanshe, 2002), p.44.

According to data collected by Chinese sociologists, it was estimated that in 1999, China's middle class was about 11 percent of the population, or around 140 million people, more than double its size twenty years earlier. The size of the middle class is greater in the more developed coastal provinces than in less developed interiors. At least 30 percent of the population in the newly industrialized city of Shenzhen in the late 1990s were professionals, such as managers, engineers, and technicians. An additional 23 percent could qualify as "white collar" workers. By comparison, the proportion of professionals is much smaller in less developed areas. In Hefei, the capital of Anhui province (one of the poorest in China), about 18 percent of the population were considered professionals and another 21 percent would qualify as "white collar" workers.[6]

Institutionally, growing social pluralism is reflected in the increase of nongovernmental organizations (NGOs) in China. This phenomenon is the product of both rising social diversity and loosening government restrictions on society. The preceding chapter by Carol Lee Hamrin and other studies have shown that NGOs have proliferated in Chinese society over the last twenty years and are playing an important role, especially in providing organized leisure activities, social services, and environmental protection.[7] However, authoritarian rule limits the growth of social pluralism. In the Chinese case, most NGOs continue to operate under severe political restrictions. Organizations with political potential, such as religious groups and free labor unions, are banned. Registration and approval processes are unduly burdensome. However, in spite these adverse conditions, China has seen the growth of (underground) religious groups and small independent labor unions. The Falun Gong spiritual movement, banned by the government in 1999 as an "evil cult," is perhaps the most illustrative example of the rising appeal of religious or quasi-religious movements among the Chinese population.

SOCIAL AND PHYSICAL MOBILITY

Economic modernization and declining state control have greatly increased the social and physical mobility of the Chinese people. Although economic forces have played a key role in the rising social mobility in China, the most crucial factor is political. During the Mao years, Chinese society was essentially an *ascriptive* society that artificially divided its members according to political criteria. Owners of land, shops, or factories, as well as those with ties to the old Kuomintang regime, were labeled "class enemies" and treated harshly. Their offspring and relatives were denied educational and professional opportunities. The Maoist regime also banned private firms, thus closing the routes of upward social mobility for nearly all entrepreneurs, regardless of social background. Deng Xiaoping's reforms abolished these policies in the 1980s.

As a result, all segments of Chinese society, particularly those groups persecuted under Maoist rule, found more economic opportunities. Market reforms forced a significant loosening of the restrictions on internal migration, allowing more than 100 million rural residents to move to more developed coastal regions in search of higher-paying jobs in the industrial and service sectors. In comparison, China's growing economy may have made a secondary contribution to the increase in social and physical mobility. Its primary contribution has come in the form of improvement in transportation, falling costs of travel, and rising income. (See table 4.2.)

A powerful force that has propelled social change in China is the unfolding information revolution. Official data in table 4.3 reflects the magnitude of this revolution since 1979. While there is little doubt that such expansion of access to information has increased the amount of information available to Chinese citizens, the political effects of the information revolution are not yet significant. The CCP retains tight control over the Chinese official media and has attempted to restrict the reach and content of new means of communications, particularly the Internet.[8] Government restrictions, coupled with the closed political process, make it more difficult for a more informed citizenry to convert information into political power. However, there are signs that the emerging information revolution, with the commercialization of the media and the spread of the Internet, is beginning to have some impact on government behavior. In some instances, the force of public opinion forced the government to be more responsive. In the age of the Internet, for example, it has become increasingly difficult for local officials to conceal major corruption scandals or serious industrial or traffic accidents. Many such stories were initially carried on the Internet and spread quickly nationwide. In most instances, an embarrassed government was forced to take action.

Table 4.2. Rising Physical Mobility in China (1978–1999).

Year	1978	1999
Passengers Transported (billion)	2.54	13.93
Private Citizens Traveling Overseas (million)	n.a.	8.92

Sources: *China's Statistical Digest 2000*, p. 122; *Law Yearbook of China, 1991*, p. 36; *Law Yearbook of China 2000*, p. 122.

Table 4.3. Expanding Access to Information (1978–1999).

Year	Number of Telephone Lines (million)	Number of Domestic Long-Distance Calls (billion)	Number of Television Sets (per 100 households)	Copies of Newspapers Printed (billion)	Number of Titles of Books Published
1978	1.9	0.18	0.3	12.8	14,987
1999	108.8	19.40	103.0	31.8	141,831

Sources: *China Statistical Digest 2000*, pp. 83, 131, 161; *Statistical Yearbook of China 1991*, p. 269.

LINKAGES TO THE OUTSIDE WORLD

China's international ties have blossomed since the late 1970s. The explosive growth of trade, cultural and educational exchanges, and tourism has enabled ordinary Chinese to forge individual contacts with the international community. Over the last two decades, 458,000 Chinese students and scholars have studied in Western universities, and 135,000 have returned to China.[9] Many have risen rapidly within the Chinese government, universities, and research institutions. This pool of new talent could play a critical role in the future transformation of China. Even those who have chosen to remain in the West have begun to contribute to the reform process in China, either through short-term visits or commercial ties. Expanding contact with the outside world provides Chinese society independent sources of information and economic support. It is likely that knowledge acquired through commerce and cultural or educational exchanges will be valuable for future reforms. China's dissidents have also benefited from these growing international ties. In some instances, this severely persecuted group was able to use these ties to publicize their cases and gain international support (including financial assistance).

CHANGES IN THE CHINESE POLITICAL SYSTEM

By comparison, changes in Chinese political institutions seem to have lagged significantly behind those in the economy and society. However, this assessment does not completely negate several important, albeit tentative, institutional reforms that are beginning to transform China's political landscape. Although the primary motive for China's post-Mao leaders to launch market-oriented reforms was to salvage a regime severely damaged by the radical policies under Maoist rule, these leaders were aware that for economic reform to succeed, some limited political reforms would have to be made. Over the past two decades, the most significant institutional changes were the strengthening of the legislative branch, development of a modern legal system, and experiments in village elections.

STRENGTHENING THE LEGISLATIVE BRANCH

The post-Mao regime initially sought to revive the legislative branch, officially known as the National People's Congress (NPC), in order to have a better division of labor in policy making at the central level. Its goal was *not* to develop alternative centers of political power. Over time, however, efforts to enhance this branch of government acquired political momentum of its own, as legislative bodies at the national and local levels were staffed with retired CCP officials who were not shy about wielding their considerable residual political influence in their new capacities. Because the 1982 Constitution gives the legislative branch considerable nominal constitutional powers and legislative capabilities, the assertion of these institutional prerogatives was fully legitimized and became more frequent.

As a trend, legislative autonomy has become very visible at the national level in recent years, and the NPC can no longer be treated as a mere "rubber stamp." In some (though rare) instances, the NPC has used its procedural rules to block decisions already made by the other two key political players, the CCP and the State Council (cabinet) until significant compromises were made (as in the case of the bankruptcy law in the mid-1980s and the imposition of the fuel tax in the late 1990s). This is gradually transforming lawmaking into a process of bargaining among different institutional, bureaucratic, and political interests.[10]

In drafting legislation, the NPC has adopted a flexible approach. Its staff often consults with Chinese legal scholars and Western legal experts. New Chinese criminal, civil, and administrative laws have borrowed extensively from Western legal doctrines, concepts, and provisions. From 1979 to 1998, the NPC passed 222 new laws, about a third of which were economic laws. Like their Western counterparts, Chinese legislative bodies have demonstrated incipient populist tendencies. National and local legislators often criticize government bureaucracies publicly for inefficiency, abuse of power, and corruption. In numerous instances, legislators took up individual cases of miscarriage of justice and environmental causes and pressed government bureaucracies for action and remedies. In China's political system, the legislative branch offers a slim ray of hope for some citizens victimized by abusive officials. With the infusion of better educated and younger legislators, Chinese legislatures are likely to grow more important and independent in the policy-making process.

LEGAL REFORM

Building a modern legal system was considered a top priority by the post-Mao government mainly because such a system would be indispensable in the pursuit of economic reforms. Investments and commercial transactions require a legal framework that was nonexistent at the end of the 1970s. China's senior leaders, therefore, including some leading conservatives (such as Peng Zhen, the head of the NPC), pushed vigorously for the adoption and implementation of new legislation. Especially noteworthy is the passage and implementation of laws regulating the financial system, the fiscal system, contract enforcement, foreign investment, accounting standards, and private enterprises. Over time, legal reform has spread to other areas, as new administrative and criminal laws have been adopted.

Although these efforts have not yet established a modern legal system, they constitute a significant first step toward building a legal framework conducive to the protection of individual and property rights. Admittedly, the effects of China's legal reform remain a subject of dispute. Some scholars question whether rule of law is feasible under an authoritarian regime and doubt the effectiveness of the post-Mao leadership's efforts to promote legal reform. Such skeptics point to Chinese press reports of ineffective enforcement, corruption in the judiciary, and lack of judicial autonomy as evidence that the progress in China's legal reform may be exaggerated. But there are also signs indicating China's new legal framework is starting to have an impact on the way in which commercial and social disputes are being addressed.

Data on trends in commercial, civil, and administrative litigation show explosive increases in the number of lawsuits filed in Chinese courts. (See table 4.4.) Rising litigation rates suggest that courts are increasingly viewed by the Chinese people and economic actors as institutions where

Table 4.4. Growth of Litigation, 1978–2000 (Cases Accepted by Courts of First Instance).

Year	Commercial	Civil	Administrative
1986	308,393	989,409	632
1990	598,314	1,851,897	13,006
1996	1,519,793	3,093,995	79,966
2000	1,297,843	3,412,259	85,760

Source: *Zhongguo falu nianjian,* various years.

social and commercial disputes may be resolved according to acceptable procedures, in spite of the many obvious flaws embedded in the emerging legal system. Finally, China's legal reform has resulted in the rapid growth of the legal profession, which was practically nonexistent at the end of the Mao era. In 2000, there were 9,500 law firms in China (approximately a third of which were private) and more than 117,000 licensed lawyers were in practice. This emerging community of legal professionals augurs well for the future of legal reform. As a specialized interest group with exten- sive ties to the courts and the legislature, legal professionals possess con- siderable political resources and a distinct professional identity. Their knowledge of the mechanisms of the legal system and self-interest could make them a significant force in consolidating the gains China has made in its legal reform.

VILLAGE ELECTIONS

The Chinese government permitted village elections largely out of political necessity in the late 1980s. After Deng's agricultural reform dismantled the communes, the state's administrative infrastructure practically collapsed, creating a political vacuum in the country's 930,000 villages where 800 million peasants lived. After rural residents began to hold unauthorized elections to form self-government in villages, both reformers and conserva- tives endorsed this experiment—for different reasons. Chinese reformers saw this experiment as the first step towards democratization, whereas con- servatives were more concerned with establishing a new mechanism of po- litical control in rural areas. The convergence of these two forces led to the passage of "The Draft Organic Law of the Village Committees" in 1987. The 1987 law was revised in 1998, and the amended law is considered to contain many procedural improvements (such as the mandatory require- ment of secret balloting).

The early history of the implementation of the village elections law was not encouraging. Between the second half of 1988 and 1989, only fourteen provinces (out of thirty) held the first round of village elections on a trial ba- sis. The political crackdown following the pro-democracy movement in Tiananmen Square in 1989 temporarily halted this reform. The experiment picked up momentum only after 1992, when a new round of economic reform was launched. At the end of 1995, twenty-four of the provinces had passed lo- cal legislation on electing village committees. According to official data, vil- lage elections have been held in all thirty provinces (excluding Tibet). By the end of the 1990s, most had completed multiple rounds of elections. Under the

Chinese Constitution, village committees elected by rural residents are not considered a form of local government. In reality, these committees manage village finance, implement government policies (such as family planning), and provide local services.

It is impossible to assess China's progress in implementing village elections on a national basis because of the short history of village elections, the diversity, and a dearth of data. Published accounts, both by academics and journalists, portray a complex but incomplete picture.[11] There are two significant hurdles to further progress. First, members of the ruling CCP seem to be disproportionately represented in elected committees. A survey of village committees carried out in the early 1990s found that about 60 percent of elected members of village committees and 50 to 70 percent of chairmen of village committees were CCP members. This has given ammunition to skeptics of China's village elections as evidence that this experiment is politically insignificant. In addition, the authority relations between the elected village committee and the unelected secretary of the CCP in villages remain unclear. The Chinese press frequently reports on village CCP bosses who interfere in the work of elected village committees. Second, elected village committees also face political interference from unelected township governments that claim direct jurisdiction over them. In several reported instances, township officials illegally nullified election results or removed elected village leaders.

Studies of village elections suggest that the success of the experiment is not related to the level of economic development. The two provinces considered leaders in this experiment, Fujian and Liaoning, are among the upper-middle income provinces. Guangdong province, one of the wealthiest, is a latecomer. There is evidence that the poorest provinces tend to lag behind wealthier ones in implementing village elections. A senior government official credited with promoting village elections suggested that successful implementation depended largely on leadership provided by provincial authorities in charge of local elections and by consistent government efforts to enforce and improve electoral procedures.[12]

REFORM AND DISCONTENTS

On balance, China's social change and limited political reforms have not fundamentally altered the authoritarian nature of the Chinese political system. The CCP's determination to preserve its political supremacy precludes several key reform measures, such as the establishment of legitimate opposition parties, competitive elections, and the formation of organized civil society groups. Therefore, the post-Mao regime's efforts to open up Chinese society and the political system have inherent limits. Of course, at the initial stage of reform, these limits were less visible and did not constitute a serious obstacle to further progress. But twenty-three years after Deng Xiaoping launched his heroic efforts to modernize China, his reforms may have reached a new stage where additional progress critically hinges on improved protection of private property rights, supremacy of the rule of law, political accountability, transparency in market transactions, strict limits on the discretion of the ruling party, and effective anti-corruption measures. Obviously, many of these principles would require a one-party regime such as the CCP to give up many of its privileges and powers for the long-term good of the country.

Although the Chinese government has so far managed to maintain a delicate balance between market reforms aimed at sustaining economic development on the one hand and defense of the CCP's political monopoly on the other, such a balance is growing increasingly precarious. Without further political reforms, the current political institutions would become progressively less capable of providing for political stability or meeting the demands of an increasingly autonomous society. Indeed, pathologies epitomizing dysfunctional political institutions are becoming more visible in today's China.[13] The most worrisome are two trends: the decaying of the ruling party and the deterioration of state capacity. These two trends, if not reversed through a reinvigorated program of political reform, will eventually threaten the sustainability of China's economic modernization and internal stability.

POLITICAL DECAY OF THE RULING PARTY

The central cause of China's governance crisis is the political decay of the ruling CCP. This process predates Deng Xiaoping's economic reform in 1979. Under Maoist rule from 1949 to 1976, the late leader's radical policies and their devastating failures, such as the Great Leap Forward (1959–1961) and the Cultural Revolution (1966–1976), ravaged the party's ranks and destroyed its image. Even though Deng's reforms aimed at reinvigorating the party, the reform process unleashed powerful forces that have gradually eroded the socioeconomic bases of the CCP. Economically, market-oriented reforms have undermined the state's direct control over economic activities. Even though the state has maintained a monopoly in such key sectors as energy, telecommunications, heavy industries, and banking, the government has withdrawn from agriculture, light manufacturing, and most service industries. As a result, the Chinese state's share in economic output and employment has fallen sharply. (See table 4.5.)

Table 4.5. Percent Share of Industrial Output and Nonagricultural Employment in China (1978–1999).

Year		State-Owned and Controlled Firms	Collectively Owned Firms	Private and Foreign Firms
1978	Industrial Output	77.6	22.2	0.2
	Non-agricultural Employment	60.4	39.5	0.1
1999	Industrial Output	28.5	38.5	33.0
	Non-agricultural Employment	29.6	43.6	26.8

Source: *China's Statistical Digest 2000.*

Given the symbiotic relationship between a party–state and a state-dominated economy, weakening state control over the economy inevitably corrodes the organizational infrastructure of the ruling party. This trend first became evident in the rural areas, which spearheaded China's reform. As agricultural decollectivization dismantled the state's old administrative structure, the CCP saw the virtual collapse of the organizational infrastructure that had been critical to the maintenance of its authority in the countryside. The party's organizational integrity in rural areas dissipated. An internal survey conducted by the CCP in the late 1990s concluded that about half of the party's rural organizational branches were either "paralyzed" or "weak."

The same story was repeated in the urban areas in the 1990s as many debt-laden state-owned enterprises (SOEs) were liquidated. Consequently, the party's organizational framework built upon these SOEs collapsed. At the same time, China's new private firms and foreign-invested enterprises have resisted the penetration by the CCP. Nearly 90 percent of China's private firms did not have a single CCP member in 2000, and the party managed to set up party branches only in one percent of such firms.

The loss of ideological appeal has dealt the CCP another blow. Ironically, the regime's success in delivering economic benefits through market reforms, combined with China's opening to the outside world, helped discredit the orthodox communist ideology. Opinion surveys conducted in China in recent years show that only a minority of ordinary citizens identify with the values and goals of communism. Although the decline of the communist ideology allowed the leadership to adopt more pragmatic policies, it undermined the party's authority at two levels. For the Chinese people, a ruling party that lacks core values with which they can identify has little capacity to maintain popular loyalty beyond delivering acceptable economic performance. For the members of the ruling elite, erosion of core ideological beliefs breeds cynicism, opportunism, and corruption.

Over time, organizational atrophy and ideological decline have contributed to the weakening of internal discipline and accountability and resulted in rampant corruption. Recent opinion polls in China indicate that, in urban areas, corruption is viewed as the most important cause for concern, surpassing even unemployment. The Chinese public's perception that the CCP has become a corrupt, self-serving elite is one of the principal causes of the decline of the party's legitimacy.

To date, the CCP's own efforts to fight corruption have proved inadequate. Official data show that only 6 percent of CCP members found to have engaged in corrupt activities were prosecuted by the courts in the late 1990s. The CCP's inability to police itself has contributed to the emergence of a collusive local officialdom in many areas. Chinese media reports show that local officials increasingly collude with each other and engage collectively in corrupt activities. One example is the municipal government in Shenyang, capital of Liaoning province in the northeast. In the late 1990s, almost all the senior officials in the city were involved in bribe-taking and providing protection for organized crime. These are the warning signs that political rot may be spreading beyond control, especially at the lower reaches of the Chinese party–state.

DETERIORATING STATE CAPACITY

The decaying of the ruling party in a party–state directly leads to the deterioration of state capacity. As the CCP effectively fractures into a collection of personalized patronages, each of which is in pursuit of its narrow self-interests, the party–state grows progressively incapable of providing public goods, such as health, education, environmental protection, and public safety. These trends call for a reassessment of China's achievement in the last two decades. An overall decline in government performance suggests that economic growth in China may be of *low quality*. Such low-quality high growth has huge hidden costs and is ultimately unsustainable.

Deterioration in state capacity can be traced to two sources, one fiscal and the other political. The fiscal weakness of the Chinese state is well known. Official data show that the government's tax revenues have declined by half since the late 1970s, from more than 30 percent of GDP in 1978 to 14 percent of GDP in 2000. This dramatic fiscal deterioration is often blamed for the government's inability to fund social services adequately. However, this argument misstates the extent of the fiscal decline and thus misses the real cause of deteriorating state capacity. Measuring the state's fiscal health only by its nominal tax revenues overlooks other forms of revenues the government collects. In fact, the precipitous fall in tax receipts has been accompanied by an explosive rise in nontax receipts. Two types of revenues, known in China as "off-budget" and "outside-the-system," are estimated to have been between 10 and 15 percent of GDP during the late 1990s. Thus, aggregate government revenues probably remain, as a share of GDP, the same today as twenty years ago.

Any decline is modest, but a fiscal system with half of its receipts kept off the books can become extremely dysfunctional. The collection and spending of the off-the-books revenues are more subject to abuse and corruption because of the lack of transparency and control. Additionally, political incentives are structured in such a way that local governments (mainly provincial and municipal governments) with access to such revenues are motivated to spend them on inefficient or showcase projects (such as duplicate manufacturing facilities or real estate developments) that can embellish their short-term record quickly. Investments in projects with long-term social returns, such as education, health and the environment are often sacrificed.

In comparison, the political origin of China's deteriorating state capacity is an even bigger cause for concern. The country's dysfunctional fiscal system merely conceals the state's fragmenting authority. In the post-Mao era, one of the most important political developments is the progressive erosion of the political authority of the central government. The causes of this erosion are complex. To the extent that economic decentralization enhances local political power, such erosion is perhaps inevitable. Moreover, economic reform requires *administrative* decentralization, another factor in the decline of the central government's authority. This changing balance of power directly affects the state's capacity to provide public goods. Local governments with newly acquired revenues have no incentives to provide such goods because they will be consumed elsewhere (for example, a well-educated, healthy worker may find employment in another jurisdiction). At the same time, a revenue-starved central government lacks the resources to do so. Most important, China's closed political system shuts ordinary people out of the local political process, leaving these consumers of public goods with no voice in deciding how local revenues ought to be spent. As a result, China's local officialdom, insulated from central oversight from above and public pressure from below, has become unaccountable. This political environment encourages local officials to subvert public interests with impunity, eviscerating state capacity.

As already noted, China's transition from communism has been constrained by two conflicting objectives—promoting economic growth on the one hand and protecting the monopoly of the CCP on the other. These two goals are ultimately incompatible because economic growth is unlikely to be sustained in an institutional environment that lacks political accountability and secure property rights. Consequently, the inadequacies of China's semi-reformed system will grow more evident over time. Tensions caused by a growing gap between underperforming political institutions and the requirements of an increasingly open and complex economy will pose enormous challenges to China's leaders—and American policy makers.

IMPLICATIONS FOR AMERICAN POLICY

This preliminary assessment of China's transition from communist rule yields a complex and evolving picture, and offers material for both optimists and pessimists in charting China's political future. On the one hand, China has made much progress in jettisoning its totalitarian past and building a more open and pluralist society. Internally, the ruling CCP has gradually loosened its control over the economy and society. China's social and economic dynamism has gained a self-sustaining momentum that is unlikely to be reversed by reactionary policy changes by the regime. Limited political reform measures, such as strengthening the legislative branch, implementing legal reforms, and instituting village elections, constitute a basic framework upon which future democratic reforms can be based. On the other hand, the CCP has demonstrated a complete lack of willingness to share power or allow substantive institutional constraints to be placed on the exercise of its power. Its determination to perpetuate an authoritarian regime has led to both the suppression of pro-democracy opposition groups and the breakdown of political accountability within the regime that is directly responsible for the rampant corruption in China.

This mixed picture presents a difficult dilemma for American policy makers. China's rapid progress in social and economic development and emerging trends of political opening provide a strategic rationale for staying with the engagement policy of the last thirty years. To abandon this policy in favor of a more confrontational approach would not only squander the valuable political assets accumulated by past administrations, but deal a perhaps fatal blow to the future development of democratic institutions in China (since a China engaged in a hostile confrontation with the United States is much less likely to pursue a course of domestic political reform). The Bush administration's goal of promoting democratic changes in China would thus not be realized.

The continuation of one-party rule in the world's largest country and fastest-growing economy is also a cause for strategic concerns. The difference in dominant political values in the two societies, as has been the case since the end of the Cold War, is one of the principal sources of friction in bilateral relations. Tensions caused by disagreements over human rights and religious freedom undermine public support within the United States for friendly ties with China, while American criticism of China's human rights record and threats of sanctions cannot avoid antagonizing ordinary Chinese people.[14] At a geopolitical level, an autocratic China with capabilities comparable to those of the United States is more likely to challenge key American interests and become a strategic competitor. Realists thus prefer a "preemptive" containment strategy that would use the current overwhelming American strength to prevent the rise of China and eliminate a potential "peer competitor."[15]

On balance, the strategy of "hedged engagement" is a less risky strategy for the United States because a "preemptive" containment strategy is, at the moment, unnecessary, counterproductive, and costly. A complete breakdown of U.S.–China relations caused by long-term American strategic concerns without Chinese provocation or hostility would make China a determined foe of the United States and set off another major-power cold war in one of the world's hot spots. The Asian region will become less stable as the restraining influence exerted by the engagement policy on Chinese behavior disappears. China would be less likely to cooperate with the United States on issues of vital interests to the United States, such as nonproliferation of weapons of mass destruction and counterterrorism.

"Hedged engagement," however, has been too passive in the promotion of democratic changes in China. The U.S. government has taken a strong stand on human rights issues in its bilateral relations with China, but has devoted an insignificant amount of resources to the promotion of domestic institutional changes inside China that would have important long-term implications for China's political evolution. The Bush administration should expand its efforts to encourage and support democratic changes in China. The progressive trends discussed in this chapter should be the main targets for American efforts.

1. Legal reform: President Bill Clinton and Chinese President Jiang Zemin reached an agreement to assist the development of the rule of law in China in 1997, but the U.S. government has spent little money on specific initiatives. The total amount of funds spent inside China on programs related to the promotion of the rule of law was too small to make an impact (in fact, the Ford Foundation spends more money inside China each year than the U.S. government on promoting legal reform). The Bush Administration should thus significantly expand its efforts. Its recent increase in budgetary allocations for rule-of-law assistance programs in China is a promising start. But the $10 million allocation, most of which must be spent outside China due to Congressional restrictions, is insufficient (less than a penny per Chinese citizen).

2. Legislative exchanges: the Bush administration should devise and implement programs to provide assistance to China's local legislators whose political influence has grown in recent years. Such assistance efforts may include visits to American state and local legislatures, and trips by American local legislators to China. Technical expertise in drafting and passing legislation will be useful for China's inexperienced local legislators. Since many American and Chinese cities or provinces have close relations, considerations should be given to forming special ties between the legislative bodies in these "sister cities" or "sister provinces."

3. Electoral reform: American nongovernmental organizations and groups affiliated with the National Endowment for Democracy (NED) have made important contributions to assisting village elections in China. But these groups, such as the National Democratic Institute and the International Republican Institute, have insufficient resources to expand or sustain their activities. The U.S. government should also consider sending American local election officials to China to assist in improving electoral procedures and technicalities.

4. Social pluralism: As China faces a myriad of new socioeconomic challenges that its government is increasingly less capable of confronting, Chinese civil society groups, particularly those devoted to environmental protection and public health, will play a growing role. The U.S. government should use its enormous political and diplomatic resources to assist these groups in their efforts, as well as facilitate the exchange between these new Chinese groups and their American counterparts. This international civil society coalition could become an important force in changing China from the ground up.

President Bush's National Security Strategy has outlined an ambitious strategic goal—China's democratic transformation. Although this objective will elude Washington in the near to medium future, the Bush administration should continue to build on the accomplishments by previous administrations in encouraging the emergence of an open China. "Hedged engagement" remains the most promising policy to safeguard vital American interests and promote American values. But without renewed efforts and commitments, this policy will be no more than an empty slogan.

NOTES

1. Debate on U.S.–China relations covers a wide range of issues. For a survey of these issues, see Richard Betts and Thomas Christensen, "China: Getting the Questions Right," *The National Interest* 62 (winter 2000–2001): 17–29; Zbigniew Brzezin-

ski, "Living with China," *The National Interest* 59 (spring 2000): 17–21; David Lampton, *Same Bed, Different Dreams: Managing U.S.–China Relations, 1989–2000* (Berkeley: University of California Press, 2001); Robert Ross, ed., *After the Cold War: Domestic Factors and U.S.–China Relations* (Armonk, N.Y.: M. E. Sharpe, 1998); David Shambaugh, "Facing Reality in China Policy," *Foreign Affairs* 80, no. 1 (January–February 2001): 50–64; Lanxin Xiang, "Washington's Misguided China Policy," *Survival* 43, no. 3 (autumn 2001): 7–24.

2. "Introduction," *The National Security Strategy of the United States* (See appendix 3).

3. Section VIII, *The National Security Strategy of the United States*.

4. *Statistical Yearbook of China 2000*, 105.

5. *China's Statistical Digest 2000*, 37.

6. Xueyi Lu, *Dangdai zhongguo shehui jaichen yanjiu baogao* [*Research Report on Social Strata in Contemporary China*] (Beijing: Shehui kexue wenxian chubanshe, 2002), 11–12.

7. See Gordon White, Jude Howell, and Xiaoyuan Shang, *In Search of Civil Society: Market Reform and Social Change in Contemporary China* (Oxford, U.K.: Clarendon); Minxin Pei, "Chinese Civic Associations: An Empirical Analysis," *Modern China* 24, no. 3 (July 1998): 285–318.

8. Christopher Marsh and Laura Whalen, "The Internet, e-Social Capital, and Democratization in China," *American Journal of Chinese Studies* 7, no. 1 (April 2000): 61–82.

9. Xinhua News Agency, October 3, 2002.

10. For three excellent studies on the evolution of Chinese legislatures, see Murray Scot Tanner, *The Politics of Lawmaking in Post-Mao China: Institutions, Processes and Democratic Prospects* (New York: Oxford University Press, 1998); Roderick McFarquhar, "Report from the Field: Provincial People's Congresses," *China Quarterly* 155 (September 1998): 656–667; Michael William Dowdle, "The Constitutional Development and Operations of the National People's Congress," *Columbia Journal of Asian Law* 1, no. 1 (spring 1997): 1–125.

11. Many studies have been conducted on village elections, see Sylvia Chan, "Research Notes on Villagers' Committee Election: Chinese-style Democracy," *Journal of Contemporary China* 7, no. 19 (November 1998): 507–522; Larry Diamond and Ramon H. Myers, eds., *Elections and Democracy in Greater China* (New York: Oxford University Press, 2001); M. Kent Jennings, "Political Participation in the Chinese Countryside," *American Political Science Review* 91, no. 2 (June 1997): 361–372; Daniel Kelliher, "The Chinese Debate over Village Self-government," *The China Journal* 37 (January 1997): 63–86; Melanie Manion, "Chinese Democratization in Perspective: Electorates and Selectorates at the Township Level," *China Quarterly* 163 (September 2000): 764–782; Kevin O'Brien, "Accommodating 'Democracy' in a One-party State: Introducing Village Elections in China," *The China Quarterly* 162 (June 2000): 465–491; Kevin O'Brien, "Implementing Political Reform in China's Villages," *Australian Journal of Chinese Affairs* 32 (July 1994): 33–60; Tian-Jian Shi, "Village Committee Elections in China: Institutionalist Tactics for Democracy," *World Politics* 51, no. 3 (November 1999).

12. Interview with Zhengyao Wang, official in the Ministry of Civil Affairs.

13. See Minxin Pei, "China's Governance Crisis," *Foreign Affairs* 81, no. 5 (September–October 2002): 95–106.

14. According to a poll of 5,700 residents in eleven cities in 1998 conducted by a Beijing-based private polling firm, Horizon Research, about 27 percent cited American criticisms of China's human rights record as the cause of their resentment against the United States; American support for Taiwan was cited by 25 percent as a source of their resentment. See Xin Ru et al., eds., *Zhongguo shehui xinshi fengxi yu yuche 1999* (Beijing: Shehui kexue wenxian chubanshe, 1999), 114.

15. See John Mearsheimer, *The Tragedy of Great Power Politics* (New York: Norton 2001).

5

Chinese Nationalism and Its Foreign Policy Ramifications

Suisheng Zhao

During the April 2001 standoff over the collision between an U.S. EP-3 re-conaissance plane and a Chinese fighter jet, the front page headline of the *Washington Post* read: "New Nationalism Drives Beijing."[1] Although perhaps exaggerated, such a warning reflects the fact that nationalism (or patriotism, *aiguozhuyi*, in the official Chinese lexicon), is indeed on the rise as a power-ful force in China. It is not only openly promoted by the communist state, it is also advocated by many Chinese intellectuals, liberals and conservatives alike, and is even reflected in the popular mood.

THE RESURGENCE OF CHINESE NATIONALISM AFTER THE COLD WAR

The remarkable resurgence of Chinese nationalism after the end of the Cold War can be observed on least three levels: state, among intellectuals, and within popular society.

The Top-Down Promotion of Patriotism by the Communist State

After the end of the Cold War, the rapid decay of communist ideology became a grave concern of the Chinese Communist Party (CCP). As faith in communism declined and citizens lost confidence in the communist regime, the CCP redis-covered the utility of nationalism. The sanctions against China by Western coun-tries after the 1989 Tiananmen crackdown ironically provided an opportune mo-ment for the communist regime to position itself as the representative of Chinese national interests and the defender of Chinese national pride against Western sanctions, which were interpreted as anti-China rather than anti-Communist.

One of the most important actions taken to promote state-led nationalism in China has been the launching of an extensive propaganda campaign of patriotic education shortly after the 1989 crackdown. This campaign appealed to national pride in the name of patriotism to ensure loyalty among a population that was otherwise significantly discontent. It redefined the legitimacy of the post-Tiananmen leadership in a way that would permit the Communist Party's rule to continue on the basis of a non-Communist ideology. In a way, the campaign deliberately blurred the lines between patriotism, nationalism, socialism, and communism. As CCP General Secretary Jiang Zemin said, "in China today, patriotism and socialism are unified in essence."[2]

The core of the patriotic education campaign was the so-called *guoqing jiaoyu* (education in national essence or national conditions), which unambiguously held that China's *guoqing* (national conditions) was unique and not ready for adopting Western-style liberal democracy. Instead, one-party rule should continue because it would help maintain political stability, which was a pre-condition for rapid economic development.

While the contents of patriotic education were wide-ranging, three themes dominated the campaign: (1) Chinese tradition and history; (2) territorial integrity; and (3) national unity. Chinese tradition, which was under fierce attack by the communist state for many years, now held a prominent place in patriotic education. Chinese history was characterized by its unceasing efforts to improve itself and to struggle against foreign aggression and oppression after repeated setbacks. The CCP linked communist China with its noncommunist past and defined patriotism in terms that had everything to do with Chinese history and culture and almost nothing to do with imported Marxist dogma. While the Great Wall in northern China was celebrated as an armory of official patriotism,[3] the Humen Burning Opium site in Guangdong province reminded the Chinese people of the beginning of "the hundred years of suffering and humiliation in the hands of foreign imperialism."[4] The celebration of the Great Wall and many historical sites was accompanied by the revival of Confucianism and other traditional Chinese cultural activities. The communist state stressed certain Confucian values of propriety in relationships, such as social hierarchy and harmony of interests, to tell the Chinese people to be loyal and obedient to the state.

The patriotic education campaign also emphasized national pride and territorial integrity. In the midst of the Western sanctions, the Chinese communist regime made the accusation that "a small number of Western countries feared lest China should grow powerful, thereby exercised sanctions against her, contained her, and added great pressures on her to pursue Westernization and disintegration (*xihua he fenhua*)."[5] The Communist regime warned of the existence of hostile international forces in the world perpetuating imperialist insult to Chinese pride. Patriotism thus was used to bolster CCP leadership in a country that was portrayed as besieged and embattled. Defending China's national interests, the communist regime presented itself as the fighter for China's entry into the World Trade Organization (WTO), the maintenance of the Most Favored Nation (MFN) status or the Permanent Normal Trade Relations (PNTR) in the United States, and the hosting of the Olympic Games in Beijing.

A third theme of patriotic education was national unity against ethnic separatist movements, which were among the myriad social and political problems confronting the Chinese communist leaders in the post–Cold War era. The central point in this theme was that the Han and ethnic minorities are inseparable from each other. The Party wanted to cultivate the idea among people of all nationalities that "the Han nationality cannot do without ethnic minorities and vice versa, so that they will consciously safeguard national unity and the motherland's unification."[6] The national unity theme was particularly emphasized in ethnic minority concentrated areas, such as Tibet, Xinjiang, and Inner Mongolia, where so-called narrow-nationalism or separatism was targeted in the campaign. The Chinese nation was said to have a great power of national cohesiveness (*ningjuli*). Many books on the Chinese national cohesiveness were published as texts of patriotic education.

To a great extent, the patriotic education campaign served its purposes. Although many Chinese people, particularly educated intellectuals, had distrusted the official propaganda and tried to read between the lines for many years, many of them accepted the core themes of the patriotic education campaign. As Liu Xiaobo observed, "No government sponsored patriotic campaign . . . can compare with the latest surge in patriotism in the suddenness with which it occurred in its intensity, and in its longevity. It seems that the wound of national humiliation inflicted on China in the past one hundred years has been reopened."[7]

The Intellectual Discourse on Nationalism

At the intellectual level, the mainstream of Chinese intellectual discourse experienced a drastic shift from enthusiastic worship of the West in the 1980s to deep suspicion of the West in the 1990s. This shift of discourse came largely as a result of the discovery of China's new position and the reassessment of China's national interests shaped by geopolitical conflicts in the post–Cold War world. As Strobe Talbott highlighted in chapter 1, China was a friendly and strategic partner of the United States in the triangular competition with the Soviet Union during the last years of the Cold War. After the disintegration of the Soviet Union, China was left as the only major communist power in the world and, to an extent, replaced the Soviet Union as the communist "evil empire" in the eyes of some American politicians. As a result, China's relations with major Western countries, particularly the United States, experienced a dramatic change after the end of the Cold War due to the disputes over the issues of human rights, intellectual property rights, trade deficits, weapons proliferation, and Taiwan. This change of position forced Chinese intellectuals to look at the United States and other Western countries in a more realistic perspective.

Many Chinese intellectuals were particularly sensitive to the views expressed by some Western intellectuals writing in the post–Cold War period. Three works in particular were directly pertinent to China's relations with the Western world: Francis Fukuyama's *The End of History and the Last Man*, Samuel P. Huntington's *The Clash of Civilizations?*, and Richard Bernstein and Ross H. Munro's *The Coming Conflict with China*.[8] While some Chinese liberal intellectuals welcomed Fukuyama's argument in terms of the victory of liberalism, they were not sure if the Western liberal democracies would not come to confront China's rise in the post–Cold War world. Their concern was confirmed by Huntington's argument that geopolitical struggles after the Cold War were not ideologically motivated but defined by civilizational differences. They were thus convinced that a confrontation between different nation–states under the banner of nationalism was going to replace the opposition between communism and capitalism. Chinese intellectuals were particularly apprehensive about Huntington's prediction that the biggest threat to Western civilization came from Islamic and Confucian cultures. This prediction drew vociferous attacks from Chinese intellectuals who argued that any future conflicts would be over national interests and the thesis of civilizational clash was little more than a guise for clashes of national interests. Under these circumstances, some Chinese intellectuals argued that nationalism would be indispensable and a rational choice to advance China's national interests.[9] This line of thinking became an important theoretical basis upon which Chinese intellectual discourse on nationalism was developed.

In response to the alarming message that there was a Western conspiracy to contain China, some Chinese intellectuals began to write articles and books advocating nationalism. Although to a certain extent the emerging intellectual discourse on nationalism overlapped with the patriotic education rhetoric of the Chinese government, its emergence was largely independent of official propaganda. Those who contributed to the intellectual discourse on nationalism were from various political backgrounds. As Wang Xiaodong (using the name Shi Zhong) observed, "Among those under the banner of nationalism, there is a full array of people: some of whom advocate authoritarianism, others who support expansionism; while some people believe in more state controls, and others uphold the total freedom in the market economy. There are also those who propose a return to tradition and others opposing this restoration."[10] The important common denominator that brought together intellectuals of different political views was the concern over China's changing position in the post–Cold War world. Immediately after the 1989 Tiananmen incident, the anti-Western speeches of He Xing, a scholar in the Chinese Academy of Social Sciences, were almost totally ignored by most intellectuals because he was seen as merely repeating the words of the authorities. This situation changed quickly after the disintegration of the Soviet Union in 1991.[11] More and more mainstream Chinese intellectuals joined the debate about the cultural identity of China in contrast with the Western civilizations and became critical of Western mainstream values and cultural colonialism.

To a certain extent, the shift in intellectual discourse resulted from the more frequent and widespread exchanges of Chinese intellectuals with the West, especially with the United States. These exchanges helped demystify Western modernization models and gave them the courage and ammunition to criticize Western cultures and societies from a more realistic perspective. In Xiao Gongqin's words, "after the opening of China to the outside world in the late twentieth century, Chinese intellectuals judged the world more and more by secular rationality rather than utopian versions of the future."[12] A nationalist discourse emerged after Chinese intellectuals became increasingly realistic in their understanding of the Western countries and world power relations in the post–Cold War era.

Nationalist Sentiment in the Popular Society

Nationalism was not the sole province of state propaganda and intellectual discourse; populist sentiments were also part of the nationalist orchestra. This was expressed vividly by a series of instant bestsellers—known as the "say no" books—published in the mid-1990s. These popular books, according to a Chinese scholar, used "extreme words" (*jiduanhua de huayu*) and expressed the "emotion of a large number of people in Chinese society."[13]

The first of the popular "say no" books was *Zhongguo Keyi Shuo Bu* (*The China That Can Say No*), authored by a group of young journalists. It aroused keen interest among many Chinese people and became an instant bestseller, selling more than two million copies in 1996. The book warned that the U.S.–led Western countries were organizing an "anti-China club," and called on China to say "no" to various unreasonable demands from the West and criticized the lack of a nationalist consciousness (*quefa minzu yishi*) among the Chinese themselves. The authors claimed, "the nineteenth century was the century of humiliation for the Chinese. The twentieth century has been the century that the Chinese experienced all kinds of sufferings in mankind . . . the twenty-first century will be the century for the Chinese to restore its glory."[14]

After the publication of *The China That Can Say No*, others soon appeared, such as *Zhongguo Hai Shi Neng Shuo Bu* (*The China That Still Can Say No*), *Zhongguo Heyi Shuo Bu* (*How China Can Say No*), and *Renminbi Keyi Shuo Bu* (*Chinese Currency Can Say No*).[15] In addition to the books with straightforward "say no" titles, many other books that depicted a confrontational relationship between China and the West were published in the mid-1990s and became integral parts of the "say no" series.[16] These books tried to show that it was the United States that forced China time and again into a series of confrontations with it and warned Washington that any containment effort was certain to fail since China was growing in strength. Filled with emotion, these books carried a simple yet heavy message to the Chinese people: morally corrupt Western countries, particularly the overstretched United States, were plotting against China in a new cold war. As a result, it was necessary and almost mandatory for China to stand up and say no clearly and loudly to these hostile foreign countries.

One interesting phenomenon in relation to the upsurge of nationalism at the popular level was the rise of "Mao Fever" in the 1990s. The communist dictator, Mao Zedong, was praised in popular books as a "great patriot and national hero" because of his courage to stand firm against Western imperialism. Mao's thought was attributed to the rise of China, as indicated by the title of a book, *Mao Zedong Sixiang yu Zhongguo de Jueqi* (*Mao Zedong Thought and the Rise of China*).[17] Books on Mao's life once again became popular among the Chinese youth.[18] Stuart R. Schram's book written in 1969, *The Political Thought of Mao Tse-Tung*, was translated into Chinese and published in 1987.[19] Although it did not sell well during the first four years after its publication, it suddenly became popular and sold over 240,000 copies in 1991.[20] Many Western visitors to China in the 1990s were impressed by the display of Mao's statues and pictures in almost all taxicabs. Mao buttons also became fashionable among many Chinese people. In an attempt to explain "Mao Fever," it was suggested that Chinese people were beginning to think about "what was China's national spirit." It was concluded that "China's problems have to be resolved by the Chinese people. China's national interests should be the first priority for the nation. In this case, the Chinese people were reminded of and came to re-appreciate Mao Zedong's struggle and accomplishments for national self-strengthening (*minzu ziqiang*) and independence." According to this work, the "high tide of Mao fever" came from the Chinese people's rediscovery of "Mao's love of the masses, Mao's lasting charisma, Mao's determination to reverse China's backwardness, and Mao's contribution to national self-strengthening."[21] A Western scholar also indicated that the nostalgia for Mao was to a great extent a reflection of the populist sentiment of nationalism.[22]

FOREIGN POLICY IMPLICATIONS
OF CHINESE NATIONALISM

Whiting argued in his 1983 study that China had experienced a transition from an affirmative nationalism, which emphasized an exclusive but positive "us," to an assertive nationalism by adding a negative "them." But Whiting did not find any imputation of belligerence or aggression attached to his concept of assertive nationalism.[23] In a 1987 study, Michel Oksenberg developed a four-category topology of Chinese nationalism: (1) xenophobic nationalism, (2) emotional nationalism, (3) assertive nationalism, and (4) confidential nationalism. Oksenberg believed that Chinese leaders in the post-Mao era were featured as confidential nationalism. He confirmed Whiting's argument by pointing out that "the leaders of modern China have not exhibited the ultra or expansionist nationalism that so many rising powers have manifested."[24] Although China rose as a world economic powerhouse in the 1990s, some scholars still held the view that Chinese nationalism would not become a source of international aggression. Yongnian Zheng suggested strongly that aggressive Chinese nationalism was a misperception of the West.[25] Erica Strecher Downs and Phillip C. Saunders also argued that "concerns about aggressive Chinese nationalism are overstated, or at least premature."[26] Whiting later became cautious, however, and in his 1995 study he was not sure if Chinese nationalism would not become aggressive.[27]

Some other scholars took a step further and described Chinese nationalism in the 1990s as a dangerous new nationalism that could drive a rising China into an aggressive stance. Ying-shih Yu stated that old Chinese nationalism was derived from an instinct of survival and therefore was defensive in nature while new Chinese nationalism is derived from China's wealth and power and is hence aggressive. Yu believed that Chinese "new nationalism" is aimed at "replacing the dominant position of the West in the world and making the twenty-first century a Chinese century."[28] Edward Friedman characterized new Chinese nationalism as a type of chauvinism. He believed that "far from acting in line with Mao's anti-imperialist nationalism . . . China's 1990s chauvinists who insist on a quick timetable for Taiwan's return to the PRC have self-consciously turned against Mao's nationalism."[29] In the meantime, Bernstein and Munro warned, "Driven by nationalist sentiment, a yearning to redeem the humiliations of the past, and the simple urge for international power, China is seeking to replace the United States as the dominant power in Asia."[30] Samuel P. Huntington also pointed out that Chinese in the 1990s increasingly asserted their intention to resume the historic role of "the preeminent power in East Asia." They wanted "to bring to an end the overlong century of humiliation and subordination to the West and Japan that began with British imposition of the Treaty of Nanking (Nanjing) in 1842."[31] James

Lilley, a former U.S. ambassador to China, echoed, "there is a rallying cry for Chinese everywhere . . . that after a century of humiliation and Mao's social and economic experiments China's time has come . . . it (China) will rise in the world to the place it deserves."[32]

CONTROLLED EXPRESSION OF
ANTI-AMERICAN NATIONALISM

The relationship with the United States is the most crucial and important one in China's foreign relations. It is also the most frustrating foreign policy challenge for China's leaders. While China's pragmatic leaders have hoped to establish and maintain a "friendly and cooperative relationship" with the United States, the unwieldy superpower holding the key to China's future of economic modernization, they are also concerned that rising nationalism would evolve into a criticism of Chinese foreign policy, especially its seemingly "soft" stance toward the United States. In this case, pragmatic leaders have tried to avoid the danger of falling victim to the nationalism that they themselves have cultivated in order to ensure that Chinese foreign policy is not dictated by the emotional voice of university students and liberal nationalist intellectuals. It is not at all surprising that pragmatic Chinese leaders have described nationalism as a force that must be "channeled" in its expressions, including restraining or even banning students from holding anti-American demonstrations.

The patriotic education campaign helped nurture the mood of nationalism at the intellectual and popular levels. But pragmatic leaders quickly discovered the danger of falling victim to their own nationalist agenda. In particular, the crisis caused by the accidental bombing of the Chinese embassy by the United States on May 8, 1999 was a wake-up call. The crisis caused by the midair collision between a U.S. Navy EP-3 reconaissance plane and a Chinese fighter jet over the South China Sea on April 1, 2001 further alarmed pragmatic leaders about the damage that uncontrolled nationalism could cause to China's national interests. After the bombing, the Chinese government mildly encouraged demonstrations in the front of U.S. diplomatic missions for the first couple of days. Demonstrations quickly spiraled out of control and not only threatened permanent damage to Sino–U.S. relations but also provoked domestic criticism that the leadership was unwilling to confront the United States. Pragmatic leaders learned their lesson the hard way and decided to ban unauthorized demonstrations two days after the bombing incident. When the second crisis took place, pragmatic leaders were determined to avoid a repeat of the previous situation and tried to orchestrate an official show of strong protest while making every effort to control popular expressions of nationalism.

THE LESSON FROM THE EMBASSY BOMBING CRISIS

In the wake of the U.S. bombing of the Chinese embassy in Belgrade, which killed three Chinese journalists, both Chinese government officials and average Chinese found it impossible to comprehend how NATO forces led by the United States could have bombed a Chinese embassy by mistake. NATO initially said that they had not targeted this building, but another building next to the Chinese embassy. Later, NATO changed its explanation and said that the Chinese embassy was in fact mistakenly targeted from an outdated map as a Yugoslav arms agency. Given the particular way in which the Chinese embassy was hit, the Chinese side simply could not accept NATO's explanations. They believed that the United States possessed the most advanced intelligence system in the world, allowing intelligence officers to read the numbers on automobile license plates or distinguish a women's from a man's restroom. The Chinese embassy in Belgrade was moved to its present location several years ago, giving ample time for intelligence officers to update their maps. Throughout the decades of carpet bombing during the Vietnam War, the Soviet and Chinese embassies were never hit, because the potential repercussions were considered serious. Therefore, the Chinese side would not take any "accident" explanation and held that the United States was "testing the water" for a future invasion of China.

The Chinese official media carried blanket coverage of the bombing and highly emotive stories on the Chinese victims in virulent anti-U.S. language on the first couple of days after the bombing. As soon as the bombing was reported, university students—spontaneously as well as organized by university authorities—poured into the front of the U.S. embassy in Beijing and consulates in other cities, throwing eggs and stones to express their anger at U.S.-led NATO actions. Sympathetic to the students, the police units guarding the embassy did not at first make any move to stop the demonstrations. The Chinese leadership apparently did not anticipate the vehemence of the student protests. The physical damage to the U.S. embassy and consulates spoke of the dangers of playing with nationalist fire. China's crucially important relationship with the United States could be permanently damaged by virulent nationalism unleashed in China. The price would be China's reform and economic growth, and "China would be seen as a rogue state that must be contained" by the United States and other Western countries.[33]

Indeed, encouraging or even simply tolerating popular expression of nationalism could be dangerous in China. Whether or not brainwashed by the state, the Chinese people had a strong sense of being victimized by Western powers. Such an emotion could boil over easily, particularly among students and intellectuals who were prone to turn to nationalism when they felt China

was being bullied by foreign powers. If there were an explosion of nationalist sentiment among the public, Chinese leaders could be forced to take a confrontational position against the United States, although it was not to the advantage of China's economic modernization and pragmatic efforts to adapt
China to the modern world. As Xiao Gongqin observed, "If the Pandora's box
of nationalism were opened, it could force even moderate leaders to adopt
radical policies and plunge the country into chaos. Moderate policies might
be seen as making concessions to the 'imperial West', giving hardliners an
opportunity to increase their power."[34]

This situation was obviously not in the interest of the Chinese leadership,
which sought to maintain stability as the domestic policy priority and retain a
cooperative relationship with the United States as its foreign policy priority. As
a matter of fact, pragmatic leaders had tried very hard to improve the relationship with the United States after the Tiananmen incident. Publicly, Beijing
took a strong stance in defending its position against sanctions imposed by
Western countries. Deng Xiaoping accused America of intervening in its domestic affairs and told his foreign visitors in September 1989, "China is not
afraid of sanctions, which in the long run will backfire at those imposing
them."[35] Privately, however, pragmatic leaders tried to avoid a confrontational
policy against the United States and other Western countries. At the end of
1989, Deng issued his famous twenty-four-character principle for handling
world affairs under the new situation: "Observe developments soberly, maintain our position, meet challenges calmly, hide our capacities and bide our
time, remain free of ambition, never claim leadership."[36] In November 1990,
Beijing abstained during the U.N. Security Council's vote on the use of military force against Iraq, thus freeing the way for Operation Desert Storm. When
America's power and influence were amplified by its victory in the Gulf War
and the formal demise of the Soviet Union in 1991, there was great pressure
on the Beijing leadership to launch an ideological campaign against Western
political ideas and the Soviet leaders' betrayal of socialist principles. However,
pragmatic leaders defended against the pressure on the ground that "China's
power and interests did not allow a confrontational relationship with Western
countries."[37] This pragmatic thinking later evolved into an official sixteen-
character principle in dealing with the United States: "enhancing confidence,
reducing troubles, expanding cooperation, and avoiding confrontation."

This nonconfrontational principle produced positive results. Although President Clinton linked China's MFN status with its human rights record in the
first year of his presidency, he was forced to reverse his position the next year
and eventually proposed a "strategic partnership" with China in his second
term. Pragmatic leaders in Beijing certainly did not want to see the embassy
bombing incident damaging this important relationship whether or not the

bombing was seen as a considerable provocation from the United States. As a result, they had to assume the difficult task of cooling down nationalist fury by calling for a reasoned response. Two days after the bombing, Vice President Hu Jintao made a televised speech in which, while extending government support to the students' patriotism, he appealed for calm and warned against extreme and destabilizing behavior.[38] Frenzied demonstrations quickly ran out of steam. A tight police cordon was put up around the embassy where U.S. Ambassador James Sasser and his staff had been under virtual siege for almost four days. Only small groups of protestors were allowed to enter under escort, "the police made them leave their stones behind and wouldn't allow them to throw them, and they were only allowed to stop at the gates of the embassy for one or two minutes."[39]

When an increased police presence outside the U.S. embassy showed that the Chinese government was determined to prevent protest that might agitate the United States, the Chinese media stopped showing pictures of demonstrations on the streets and instead featured organized protests in schools and workplaces. In the meantime, the *People's Daily* reported that various Western countries had issued advisories against traveling to China, hurting tourism and foreign investment.[40] In this case, although the government continued to demand that the United States engage in a thorough investigation, promptly publish the results, and punish those responsible, the official Xinhua Agency promptly listed apologies by U.S. President Bill Clinton and other NATO leaders, and state television carried Clinton's public apology. The state media also mentioned a trip made by Secretary of State Madeleine Albright to the Chinese embassy in Washington to apologize. Finally, President Jiang Zemin stated on May 11 that life in China should now return to normal and that it was time to turn a new page in the name of economic necessity: "The Chinese people have expressed their strong indignation in various forms. . . . This has demonstrated the enthusiasm, will and power of the great patriotism of the Chinese people. . . . The whole country is now determined to study and work harder, so as to develop the national economy continuously, enhance national strength, and fight back with concrete deeds against the barbaric act of U.S.-led NATO."[41]

Premier Zhu Rongji, who was criticized for making excessive concessions to the United States over Chinese accession to the WTO during his trip to Washington one week earlier, also came out to echo Jiang's statement that China would adhere to its reform and opening-up policy and "continue to develop its friendly and cooperative ties with all nations around the world."[42] It was against this background that less than one month after the bombing, Beijing restrained from vetoing the G-8 proposal (which required U.N. Security Council approval) to end the Kosovo crisis when Yugoslav leaders announced their decision to accept its conditions.[43] This was striking to some observers because, after the bombing, Beijing threatened all kinds of restrictions on U.N. Security Council activity but now did nothing. To express goodwill to U.S. leaders, President Jiang sent his congratulations to the U.S. women's soccer team after its July 10 victory over the Chinese team in the Women's World Cup final. This congratulation was reported prominently in the Chinese media and was said to be a signal that Beijing was ready to move past the incident.[44] Beijing's pragmatic policy paid off. Six months after the incident, China and the United States reached a historic agreement on the terms of China's accession to the WTO.

MANAGING THE MIDAIR COLLISION CRISIS

A midair collision between a U.S. Navy EP-3 reconaissance plane and a Chinese fighter jet over the South China Sea on April 1, 2001 created another crisis that once again highlighted the possibility of a popular explosion of nationalist sentiment. The Chinese pilot, Wang Wei, was killed in the collision and was quickly declared a "martyr of the revolution" and praised as a heroic defender of the motherland. China held the twenty-four U.S. crew members at PLA military facilities on Hainan Island for eleven days and accused the pilot of breaking the law by making an emergency landing at a Chinese air base without permission. While the collision took place in international airspace about fifty miles outside China's territorial waters, China claimed an exclusive economic zone that extends 230 miles out to sea, and asserted that the plane had no right to conduct surveillance there. Beijing sought an apology from Washington but the White House declined to apologize, saying the collision was an accident.

The spy plane incident reinforced many Chinese people's suspicion of the United States as a careless bully that threw around its weight without considering the views or feelings of people from other nations. The Chinese government did little to dispel those views. With this new incident, many Chinese became angry over American espionage, saddened by the death of a pilot, and frustrated by President Bush's unwillingness to apologize. At the root of their complaints was a sense of wounded national pride. China had suffered at the hands of foreigners before and was not prepared to suffer again. According to a news analysis by *The New York Times* shortly after the collision, "in one opinion poll on the Chinese Internet—always a hotbed of nationalist sentiment, 13,000 of 15,000 net surfers said the collision was the result of a deliberate provocation."[45] Many university students threatened that there would be larger demonstrations if the government released the crew members before the United States made an apology.[46]

In response to rising nationalist sentiments, which the communist government itself had helped cultivate earlier, all Chinese leaders had to talk tough in their standoff with Washington. While talking stiffly, however, pragmatic leaders followed a two-pronged policy, as they did not want to see a repeat of the anti-American demonstrations one year earlier. It was reported that President Jiang Zemin very quickly laid down several tough principles on how to handle the standoff at a Politburo emergency meeting moments after the collision. While there is no way for outsiders to confirm what decisions were made at this meeting, some of the principles sound plausible. One was that the American side "should offer a written apology for using its military aircraft to ram China's aircraft, resulting in a loss of a pilot, and for entering China's airspace and landing at China's airport without permission." Another was that the American side "should stop its military spying and provocative activities along China's coast." A further principle was that "China should adopt measures and be prepared against the U.S. side using the air collision incident to blackmail China politically, economically, and militarily, resulting in tension in Sino-US relations and even local confrontation."[47] However, in addition to these tough principles, the meeting also emphasized that "the leadership must protect itself from criticism by ordinary Chinese by not appearing weak before the 'hawkish' new Bush administration. Yet, at the same time, there should be no repeat of the anti-U.S. demonstrations after the 1999 NATO bombing of the Chinese embassy in Belgrade."[48]

Subsequent events proved that this emphasis was crucial in guiding the actions of Beijing's leaders during the crisis. On the one hand, Beijing's public stance was particularly uncompromising on the demand that the spy plane crew would be released only after a formal apology by the U.S. government to the Chinese people. Commentaries in major media attacked U.S. "neohegemonism" and extolled the patriotism of the Chinese people. On the other hand, pragmatic leaders ensured that the government rather than the public set the tone in determining how to deal with the United States. Beijing wanted to refrain from high-profile actions that might provoke a military confrontation with the United States. The leadership moved to censor vocal anti-American sentiment that had been pouring in on the Internet and, to some extent, in the state-run media. In Beijing and other major cities, while people's anti-American emotions ran high, the government allowed no demonstrations outside U.S. missions and no intimidation of foreign communities. To show his confidence in resolving this incident, President Jiang Zemin did not cancel an earlier scheduled foreign trip and left for a state visit to Latin America on April 4, four days after the collision. Vice President Hu Jintao was put in charge of an emergency team to handle the crisis.

Following this two-pronged policy, pragmatic leaders maintained control over the situation in Beijing's streets. As one Western reporter observed,

Unlike May 1999, when the streets were thronged with rock-throwing demon-strators and newspapers were filled with anti-American screeds, the government this time has moved swiftly to censor nationalistic rhetoric from Internet bulletin boards and keep a tighter than usual rein on the state-run press. The Beijing Youth Daily, which led the charge in 1999 with lurid photographs of mangled Chinese bodies, has so far run only two short stories on the Hainan standoff by the official New China News Agency on its front page. The only newspaper to strongly criticize the United States has been the English-language China Daily, which has limited impact.[49]

But the calm response did not mean that Chinese people's nationalist senti-ments were totally under control. As a *New York Times* reporter in Shanghai in-dicated, although "the temperature on the streets is far, far, calmer than it was after the embassy bombing, there are a few similarities though. The Chinese feeling of being a victim and being humiliated by the American bully, the dis-satisfaction with what the Chinese see as a dry, legalistic U.S. response, and the politics of the apology are important elements in this situation too."[50]

Worrying about the possibility of losing control, pragmatic leaders were eager to find a face-saving solution for both sides to get out of the crisis. For this purpose, they took a flexible position under the veneer of toughness and eventually hammered out a so-called diplomacy of apology. A Hong Kong journalist observed that, frustrated by Bush's lack of flexibility and bumbling bluntness in his initial responses, "Chinese officials began floating balloons in the form of alternative expressions that the U.S. could use to circumvent a full-fledged apology."[51] In an interview with CNN, Chinese Ambassador to the United States Yang Jiechi hinted that the United States should apologize after doing harm to China. When U.S. Secretary of State Colin Powell ex-pressed "regrets" over the loss of the Chinese pilot for the first time on April 4, the Chinese Foreign Ministry promptly responded by saying this was a "step in the right direction," while still insisting on a full apology. The next day (April 5), at a press conference in Chile, President Jiang provided a fur-ther hint by saying that it was normal for two people who had bumped into each other to say "excuse me." The U.S. side at this time also switched to a pragmatic position. President Bush expressed his regrets on the same day and, on April 9, Powell used the word "sorry" for the missing Chinese pilot and aircraft. Beijing squeezed again for something stronger than "sorry" in the next two days. When Washington said "very sorry" and indicated that it could not go any further, certainly not to the level of a full apology, Beijing ac-cepted the "very sorry" as a close equivalent to an apology on April 10 and released the crew on the next day.

It was a testimony to the pragmatic leaders' tactical flexibility that the Chi-nese official media was instructed to translate Powell's expression of "very sorry" as "*baoqian*," which is one letter different from but has almost identical meaning as "*daoqian*," the Chinese expression of "apology," which Beijing had demanded initially. Although the United States did not make a full apology to China, pragmatic Chinese leaders interpreted the expression of being "very sorry" as a full apology and the American expressions of "regrets" and "sorry" that meant in most instances only for the loss of the pilot and aircraft as meant for the whole incident. As a Western journalist suggested, "China stressed that it had forced the United States to admit its faults, as it was implicit in the usage of the character '*qian*,' which is both in *daoqian*, the apology demanded by Chinese leaders, and in *baoqian*, or deep excuses, the word used in the American statement to the Chinese." This was a face-saving solution not only for China but also for the United States. As the journalist indicated, President Bush "underscored that it did not give China the precise apology Beijing had demanded, had brought its people home, and thus was no longer subject to either possible Chinese blackmail or internal pressures over its difficulties in handling a difficult situation."[52]

Like President Bush, pragmatic Chinese leaders trumpeted the success largely for its domestic audience as they did not want to let nationalism get out of hand and hurt both the communist state and the Sino–U.S. relationship. They declared that "China had won a victory at the stage (*jieduan xing chengguo*)" in a *People's Daily* editorial on April 11, the day when Beijing released the U.S. crew. The editorial told the Chinese people that, "Our persistent struggle forced the U.S. government to change its tough and unreasonable attitudes at the beginning of the incident and finally apologized to the Chinese people. . . . This struggle extended justice, defeated the hegemonism, defended our country's sovereignty and national dignity, and demonstrated the big-nation spirit (*daguo fengmao*) of China in defending world peace and fearless in the fact of great power threat." It in the meantime stressed the importance of maintaining a cooperative relationship with the United States: "What direction will the Sino–U.S. relationship go is crucially important (*zhiguan zhongyao*) for the whole world. . . . The improvement of relationship between China and the United States is not only in the interests of the two countries but also to the advantage of world peace and stability."[53]

Apparently, while pragmatic leaders did not alter their tough rhetoric for domestic reasons, they did almost everything they could from their perspective to avoid confrontation and maintain the framework of long-term cooperation with the United States during the two crises. This seemingly contradictory strategy of talking tough but acting in a calculated manner demonstrated that the pragmatic leaders were willing to move forward to rebuild and expand interactions with the West in general, and the United States in particular, given their understanding of China's vital interests.

They recognized that China's modernization inevitably depended on adapting to the modern world and required maintaining cooperation with the U.S. and other Western countries.

Of course, their commitment to cooperation is not endless, as these leaders are both pragmatists and nationalists and constrained by the rise of Chinese nationalist sentiments. Although China remains under the rule of the Communist Party and its leaders, as the preceding chapters have argued, it is no longer headed by a charismatic dictator like Mao Zedong or Deng Xiaoping who had the authority to arbitrate disputes in the leadership or personally set the country's course. Post-Deng leaders must cater to a range of constituencies. As a result of reform and opening up, they have become far more accountable than in the pre-reform years because the average Chinese is plugged into information by phone and the Internet and has found ways to express their views, including nationalist feelings. As one Western reporter pointed out, "while voting is only possible in local elections, the increasingly loud voices of the people weigh heavily on national leaders. . . . There is definitely public opinion now."[54] Although pragmatic leaders remained in full control and did not let nationalism get out of hand during the two crises of 1999 and 2001, it remains to be seen how long this type of authoritarian control can last.

CONCLUSION

While Chinese pragmatic nationalism was reactive to threats to the communist state from both external and internal sources, it was also constrained by the same threats because these threats dictated what viable nationalist policy options were available to pragmatic leaders. As a result, pragmatic nationalism is more defensive than aggressive. That is why David Shambaugh characterized Chinese nationalism as "defensive nationalism," which "is assertive in form, but reactive in essence."[55]

The notion of defense in the Chinese case, however, needs qualifying. It is not only a matter of *external* defense or *territorial* defense, as the term is usually defined in Western security studies literature. Rather, perhaps more importantly, it is *internal* defense, because the threat to China's national security comes from both sides of its national borders. What worries Chinese communist leaders most are the liberal anti-government and ethnic separatist movements within the Chinese territory. That is why the National Defense Act passed by the National People's Congress in March 1997 stressed that one of the major functions of national defense was to prevent any split of the nation—a mission that made internal threat a primary concern of national defense.[56] For defensive purpose, Chinese leaders have embraced and depended on the Western notion of sovereignty and become very sensitive to any interference in Chinese "domestic affairs" by foreign powers. This defensive posture may be misinterpreted as aggressive behavior because China was sometimes overly sensitive about its national sovereignty. Bernstein and Munro were correct in that "China is quick to take offense and to view disagreements that other countries might take more easily in stride as assaults on national dignity, requiring uncompromising response."[57]

By reacting strongly against so-called interference in China's domestic affairs by the Western powers, pragmatic leaders really intend to defend the authority of the communist party. They play upon a perhaps exaggerated history of painful Chinese weakness in the face of Western imperialism, territorial division, unequal treaties, invasion, anti-Chinese racism, and social chaos, because the regime has to claim legitimacy based upon its ability to defend China's territorial integrity and to build a modernized Chinese nation–state. Thus, while defending its position against sanctions imposed by Western countries, pragmatic leaders in Beijing had managed to avoid a confrontational policy against the United States and other Western countries because China's vital national interest in modernization required them to keep at least workable relations with these countries. The holy principle of pragmatic nationalist leaders in the post–Cold War world is Deng's twenty-four-character principle. Following this principle, pragmatic leaders have tried to avoid confrontation while fighting for China's rightful place. As a *Reuters* report suggested in the wake of China's winning the bid for 2008 Olympic Games, "Chinese leaders are now basking in what they see as long-overdue international acceptance of China's status as a great power. . . . A China that imagines it has gained the acceptance and respect of the world may be less inclined to believe that plots are being hatched in the West, particularly the United States, aimed at subverting its political system and blocking its economic rise."[58]

It should be pointed out that a more irrational and aggressive nationalism may yet prevail in China, in which case its foreign policy would turn in a confrontational direction. But this is only one possible scenario and not an inevitability. In the twenty-first century, the United States and the rest of the international community should focus their efforts on preventing such an eventuality by helping China create an environment that will reduce its feelings of insecurity and increase its feelings of healthy self-respect—one of the foundations of democracy.

NOTES

1. John Pomfret, "New Nationalism Drives Beijing: Hard Line Reflects Popular Mood," *Washington Post*, 4 April 2001, A01.

2. Lizhi Ming, "Jianchi Aiguo Zhuyi yu Shehui Zhuyi de Tongyi" ("Insist on the Unification of Patriotism and Socialism"), *Qiushi* (Seeking the True), no. 9 (1990): 15.

3. For one excellent description on how the CCP used the Great Wall for patriotic education purpose, see Arthur Waldron, "Scholarship and Patriotic Education: The Great Wall Conference, 1994," *The China Quarterly* 143 (September 1995): 844–850.

4. This author visited the Patriotic Education Base of the Humen Opium Burning Site in 1996.

5. Quoted from Deng Xiaoping Theory Research Center, Chinese Academy of Social Sciences, "Wusi Yundong de lishi yiyi" (Great Historic Significance of May 4th Movement), *Guangming Ribao*, 26 April 1999, 2.

6. Zhongguo Gongchandang Zhongyang Weiyuanhui (the CCP Central Committee), "Aiguo Zhuyi Jiaoyu Dagang" (Guidelines for Education in Patriotism), *Renmin Ribao* (People's Daily), 6 September 1994, 1.

7. Xiaobo Liu, "Zibeigan qidong de aiguozhuyi" ("Chinese Patriotism Driven by Inferiority Complex"), *Kaifang* (*Open Magazine*), no. 11 (November 1994): 18.

8. Francis Fukuyama, *The End of History and the Last Man* (New York: Free Press, 1992); Samuel Huntington, "The Clash of Civilizations?," *Foreign Affairs* 72, no. 3 (summer 1993), and *The Clash of Civilizations and the Remaking of World Order* (New York: Simon & Schuster, 1996); and Richard Bernstein and Ross H. Munro, *The Coming Conflict with China* (New York: Alfred Knopf, 1997).

9. Jisi Wang, ed., *Wenming yu Guoji Zhengzhi: Zhongguo Xuezhe Ping Huntington de Wenming Chongtulun* (*Civilization and International Politics: Chinese Scholars on Huntington's Clashes of Civilization*), (Shanghai: Shanghai Renmin Chubanshe, 1995); Zhong Shi (Xiaodong Wang), "Weilai de Chongtu" ("Future Conflicts"), *Zhanlue yu Guanli*, no. 1 (1993): 46–50; Zhong Shi, "Zhongguo xiandaihua mianlin de tiaozhan" ("The Challenges to China's Modernization"), *Zhanlue yu Guanli*, no. 1 (1994); Shijie Guan, "Cultural Collisions Foster Understanding," *China Daily*, 2 September 1996, 4.

10. Zhong Shi, "Zhongguo de minzuzhuyi yu zhongguo de weilai" ("Chinese Nationalism and China's Future"), *Huaxia Wenzhai* (*China Digest*), (1996).

11. For more on the impact of the collapse of the Soviet Union on China's reform strategy, see Christopher Marsh, "Learning From Your Comrade's Mistakes: The Impact of the Soviet Past on China's Future," *Communist and Post-Communist Studies* 35 (September 2003).

12. Gongqin Xiao, "Zhongguo Minzuzhuyi de Lishi yu Qianjing ("The History and Prospect of Chinese Nationalism"), *Zhanlue yu Guanli*, no. 2 (1996): 62.

13. Jiling Xu, "Fanxifang zhuyi yu minzuzhuyi" ("Anti-Westernism and Nationalism"), in *Zhishifenzi lichang: minzu zhuyi yu zhuanxingqi zhongguo de mingyun* (*The Positions of Intellectuals: Nationalism and China's future in the Transitional Period*), eds. Ming Zhang and Shitao Li, (Changchun: Shidai Wenyi Chubanshe, 2000), 421.

14. Qiang Song, Zangzang Zhang, and Bian Qiao, *Zhongguo Keyi Shuo Bu* (Beijing: Zhonghua Gongshang Lianhe Chubanshe, 1996), 199.

15. Qiang Song, Zangzang Zhang, Bian Qiao, Zhengyu Tang, and Qingsheng Gu, *Zhongguo Hai Shi Neng Shuo Bu* (*The China that Still Can Say No*) (Beijing: Zhongguo Wenlian Chuban Gongsi, 1996); Xueli Zhang, *Zhongguo Heyi Shuo Bu* (*How China Can Say No*) (Beijing: Hualing Chubanshe, 1996); Chuan Tong, *Renminbi Keyi Shuo Bu* (*Chinese Currency Can Say No*) (Beijing: Zhongguo Chengshi Chubanshe, 1998).

16. Among them are Yonghong Hong et al., *Zhong Mei Jun Shi Chong Tu Qian Qian Hou Hou* (*U.S.–China Military Confrontations: Before and After*) (Beijing: Zhongguo Shehui Chubanshe, 1996); Laiwang Xi et al., *Da Yang Ji Feng: Liang Ge Shi Jie Da Guo De Bo Yi Gui Ze* (*The Oceanic Wing: The Games of Two World Class Nations*) (Beijing: Zhongguo Shehui Chubanshe, 1996), 2 volumes; Shan Zhang and Weizhong Xiao, *E Zhi Tai Du: Bu Cheng Nuo Fang Qi Wu Li* (*Stop Taiwan from Independence: No Promise on Not Using Force*) (Beijing: Zhongguo Shehui Chubanshe, 1996); Feng Chen, Xingyan Zhao, Zhaoyu Huang, Mingjie Yang, and Xiqing Yuan, *Zhongmei Jiaoliang Daxiezhen* (*A Depiction of Trials of Strength Between China and the United States*) (Beijing: Zhongguo Renshi Chubanshe, 1996).

17. Zhuwang Xu, Yi Liu, and Quanxing Li, *Mao Zedong Sixiang yu Zhongguo de jueqi* (*Mao Zedong Thought and the Rise of China*) (Beijing: Zhongguo Renmin Chubanshe, 1993).

18. Among these books, see, Shudong Ho, ed., *Yidai Juren Mao Zedong* (*A Giant, Mao Zedong*) (Beijing: Zhongguo Qingnian Chubanshe, 1993); Yun Zhang, *Zhongguo Lishi Mingyun de da jueze* (*The Great Decison over the Historical Fortune of China*) (Shanghai: Shanghai Renmin Chubanshe, 1994); Xingmin Xue, ed., *Zai Mao Zedong Shenbian* (*On the Side of Mao Zedong*) (Beijing: Zhonggong Zhongyang Dangxiao Chubanshe, 1993); Pengfei Qi and Jing Wang, eds., *Mao Zedong yu Gongheguo Jiangshuai* (*Mao Zedong and the Marshals and Generals of the Republic*) (Beijing: Hongqi Chubanshe, 1993).

19. Stuart R. Schram, *Mao Zedong* (Beijing: Hongqi Chubanshe, 1987).

20. Zhuwang Xu, Yi Liu, and Quanxing Li, *Mao Zedong Sixiang yu Zhongguo de jueqi* (*Mao Zedong Thought and the Rise of China*) (Beijing: Zhongguo Renmin Chubanshe, 1993), 77.

21. Yifu Song and Zhanbing Zhang, *Zhongguo: Mao Zedong Re* (*China: Mao Zedong Fever*) (Taiyuan, China: Beiyue Wenyi Chubanshe, 1993), 264–65 and 43.

22. For an English study of this "Mao Fever," see Edward Friedman, "Democracy and 'Mao Fever,'" *Journal of Contemporary China* 3, no. 6 (1994): 84–95.

23. Allen Whiting, "Assertive Nationalism in Chinese Foreign Policy," *Asian Survey* 23, no. 8 (August 1983): 913–933.

24. Michel Oksenberg, "China's Confident Nationalism," *Foreign Affairs* 65, no. 3 (1986–87): 504.

25. Yongnian Zheng, *Discovering Chinese Nationalism in China* (Cambridge, U.K.: Cambridge University Press, 1999), 2–20.

26. Erica Strecher Downs and Philip C. Saunders, "Legitimacy and the Limits of Nationalism: China and the Diaoyu Islands," *International Security* 23, no. 3 (1998): 117.

27. Allen Whiting, "Chinese Nationalism and Foreign Policy After Deng," *China Quarterly*, no. 142 (June 1995): 295–316.

28. Ying-shih Yu, "Minzuzhuyi de jiedu" (*Interpretation of Nationalism*), *Minzhu Zhongguo* (Democratic China), no. 35 (June–July, 1996).

29. Edward Friedman, "Chinese Nationalism, Taiwan Autonomy and the Prospects of a Larger War," *Journal of Contemporary China* 6, no. 14 (1997): 16.

30. Richard Bernstein and Ross H. Munro, "The Coming Conflict with America," *Foreign Affairs* 76, no. 2 (March/April 1997): 19.

31. Huntington, *The Clash of Civilizations*, 229.

32. James R. Lilley, "Nationalism Bites Back," *New York Times*, 24 October 1996.

33. Dali Yang, "In Bombing Aftermath, Cool Heads Must Prevail to Keep China Focused on Reforms," *ChinaOnline*, <www.chinaonline.com> (10 May 1999).

34. Josephine Ma, "Warning Issued on Nationalism's Foreign Policy Impact," *South China Morning Post*, 18 December 2000.

35. "Deng Xiaoping Met with Japanese Visitors," *Beijing Review* 32, no. 40, (2–8 October 1989): 5.

36. Youwei Chen, *Tiananmen Shijianhou Zhonggong yu Meiguo Waijiao Neimu* (*Inside Story of China's Diplomatic Relations with the U.S. After the Tiananmen Incident*) (Taipei: Zhongzheng Shuju, 1999), 100.

37. Jisi Wang, "Pragmatic Nationalism: China Seeks a New Role in World Affairs," *The Oxford International Review*, (winter 1994): 29.

38. In a conversation with Xiguang Li, one of the leading liberal nationalists in Beijing shortly after the embassy bombing incident, he told this author that Hu's speech reminded him of the April 26 *People's Daily* editorial that warned the students demonstrators for a possible crackdown before the Tiananmen massacre in June 1989.

39. "PRC Moves to Cool Nationalist Fury on Bombing," *AFP*, 11 May 1999.

40. Dali Yang, "In Bombing Aftermath, Cool Heads Must Prevail to Keep China Focused on Reforms," *ChinaOnline*, <www.chinaonline.com> (10 May 1999).

41. *Xinhua*, 11 May 1999.

42. *Xinhua*, 11 May 1999.

43. Weijun Liu, An Yinde, "China Did Not Threaten to Veto the G-8 Proposal," *China News Digest*, 3 June 1999.

44. In a conversation with a prominent Chinese scholar in late July 1999, he called for my attention to this subtle message sent by the pragmatic Chinese leadership.

45. Elisabeth Rosenthal, "News Analysis: Many Voices for Beijing," *New York Times*, 10 April 2001.

46. Graig, S. Smith, "Students' Unease over Weakness Could Threaten Beijing's Leaders," *New York Times*, 6 April 2001.

47. There were different reports about this Politburo meeting. Most Chinese reports said the meeting set five principles but a CNN report said three principles. For the Chinese reports, see, for example, Ren Wen: "Hu Jintao Shicha Jiefangjun Sizongbu he guofangbu tingqu yijian" ("Hu Jintao Visits Four General Headquarters of PLA and Defense Ministry to Solicit Opinions"), *Taiyangbao* (*The Sun Daily*), 6 April 2001; "Beijing Shiyao Meiguo Daoqian" ("Beijing is Determined to Ask the U.S. for an Apology"), *Duowei Xinwen She*, 6 April 2001. For the CNN report, see Willy Wo-Lap Lam, "Analysis: Behind the Scenes in Beijing's Corridors of Power," <www.cnn.com> (9 May 2001).

48. Lam, "Analysis: Behind the Scenes in Beijing's Corridors of Power."

49. John Pomfret, "New Nationalism Drives Beijing: Hard Line Reflects Public Mood," *Washington Post*, 4 April 2001, A1.

50. Graig, S. Smith, "Students' Unease over Weakness Could Threaten Beijing's Leaders," *New York Times*, 6 April 2001.

51. Lam, "Analysis: Behind the Scenes in Beijing's Corridors of Power."

52. Francesco Sisci, "Reading the Tea Leaves," *Asia Times Online*, 18 April 2001.

53. Editorial, "Ba Aiguo Reqing huawei qiangguo liliang" ("Transform the Warm Emotion of Patriotism into the Power of Strengthening the Nation"), *Renmin Ribao*, 11 April 2001, 1.

54. Rosenthal, "News Analysis: Many Voices for Beijing."

55. David Shambaugh, "Containment or Engagement of China," *International Security* 21, no. 12 (fall 1996): 205.

56. "Zhonghua Renmin Gongheguo Guofangfa" ("The National Defense Act of the People's Republic of China"), *Xinhua*, 18 March 1997.

57. Richard Bernstein and Ross H. Munro, *The Coming Conflict with China* (New York: Alfred A. Knopf, 1997), 42.

58. Reuters, "China to Deport U.S. Scholar After Conviction," 14 July 2001.

6

Encroaching on the Middle Kingdom?
China's View of Its Place in the World

June Teufel Dreyer

ESTABLISHING CHINA'S
PLACE IN THE POSTWAR WORLD

From the time of its founding in October 1949, the leaders of the People's Republic of China (PRC) were keenly aware of two things: first, the country had enemies, and second, there was a large gap between their country's military power and that of several states that were hostile to it and its government, the Chinese Communist Party (CCP). They adopted a series of strategies designed to protect the PRC that changed with perceived changes in the international configuration of forces as well as domestic considerations. The initial period involved alliance with the Soviet Union and its client states while largely excluding relations with noncommunist powers. This was dictated in part by the personality of then Soviet leader Joseph Stalin, who demanded absolute loyalty, and in part because many other powers continued to recognize the Kuomintang (KMT or Nationalist Party) headed by Chiang Kai-shek and now ensconced on Taiwan, as the sole legitimate government of China.

When Stalin died in March 1953, none of his potential successors possessed the same degree of determination to impose monolithic control over the Soviet bloc. Moreover, a large number of former colonies were becoming independent. In general, their leaders wanted no part of the Cold War and were opposed to joining either the Western or the Soviet bloc. The combination of these factors led the Chinese leadership toward a less rigid policy. The PRC attended the Bandung Conference of non-aligned states that was held in Indonesia in 1955 and played an active part in its deliberations. It enthusiastically endorsed the Bandung Conference's *Pancha Sheela*, or Five Principles of Peaceful Coexistence, which included such concepts as nonaggression, respect for sovereignty and the territorial integrity of other states, and noninterference in each other's affairs. China expressed solidarity with the Third World, suggesting an alliance of the world's have-nots and people of color. Chinese posters of the era showed a beaming Mao Zedong, in his standard gray suit and matching cap, marching at the center of a group of people clad in the sort of traditional dress they almost certainly would not be wearing on such an occasion—the Mexican representative in sombrero and serape, for example. The accompanying caption proclaimed "We have friends all over the world," its underlying message appeared to be that the PRC aspired to be the leader of the Third World.

The results of the policy adopted at Bandung were disappointing to the Chinese leadership. A number of countries were hesitant to acknowledge the PRC, given its large size and potential wealth, as a genuine Third World state. Its list of irredentist territorial grievances added to these misgivings, as did rhetoric advocating world revolution that cast doubt on how nonaligned the PRC actually was. Several countries accused Beijing of meddling in their internal affairs—such as supporting a communist movement in Burma and training antigovernment guerrillas in the Cameroons—which were strictly forbidden by the Pancha Sheela. From Beijing's point of view, the foreign policy adopted at Bandung was not serving its needs. And it was no nearer to replacing the rule of Chiang Kai-shek and his KMT over Taiwan with its own. Although the Soviet Union had made important advances in such areas as intercontinental ballistic missile technology and in launching the world's first space satellite, Sputnik, the USSR's new leaders showed no inclination to employ their country's technological advantages in the cause of expanding world communism. When Mao Zedong attempted to intimidate the government of Taiwan by bombarding small offshore islands under Taiwan's control, Nikita Khrushchev, Stalin's successor, made a speech that mentioned the Treaty of Brest-Litovsk; i.e., cautioning the need for delay in order to achieve one's eventual objectives. The Soviets also refused to back China, their ally, in a border dispute with nonaligned India in which the bulk of evidence favored the PRC's position. Not surprisingly, Mao was furious.

At the same time, it was becoming increasingly apparent that the Soviet model of development was inappropriate for the PRC's needs. A radical substitute, the Great Leap Forward, was instituted. Moscow's leaders were skeptical at the implied slight to their tutelage—correctly, as it turned out, since the result was famine and other disasters. Relations between the two countries worsened. Monolithic communism was no more, with many communist parties dividing into pro-Moscow and pro-Beijing factions. The pro-Moscow faction was almost always the larger by far. China entered a period of semi-isolation from the world scene, which became nearly total with the advent of its Great Proletarian Cultural Revolution in the mid-1960s.[1] PRC propaganda professed to see little difference between the U.S. and the USSR, regularly referring to them as "the superpower and the later-coming superpower" or "the capitalists and the revisionists." Mao suspected the two of colluding to constrain the development of the forces of true revolution, led by the PRC. In a clever allusion to European history, Chinese media accused the United States and the USSR of forming a "Holy Alliance" akin to the coalition of monarchists that in 1814 restored the ideological and territorial contours of the continent after the defeat of the French Revolution and Napoleon.

The Soviet invasion of Czechoslovakia in August 1968 provided a stark reminder that the USSR was a very dangerous enemy. Moscow's leader at the time, Leonid Brezhnev, justified the incursion by explaining that the Soviet Union had not only the right but the duty to protect socialism wherever it was threatened. Mao construed the Brezhnev doctrine, as it came to be known, as a warning to the PRC. In Chinese phraseology, Moscow had "killed the chicken (Prague) in order to warn the monkey (Beijing)." Although socialism in the PRC was not threatened by the forces of liberalism, as was the case in Czechoslovakia, the form of socialism practiced in China was markedly different from that of the Soviet Union. Chinese official sources regularly credited Mao Zedong with having brilliantly adapted socialism to the Chinese context, and often added that his adaptation could serve as a model for the Third World. Indeed, the PRC's media regularly accused the Soviet leadership of "revisionism." Should Brezhnev and his advisers decide to invade China, this heresy would provide a suitable theoretical justification.

The border skirmish of 1969 (see chapter 1) made the threat of invasion by China's powerful northern neighbor seem like a very real possibility. Moreover, it came at a time when the PRC was in a particularly weak position. The equipment of the Chinese military, the People's Liberation Army (PLA), had deteriorated after the break with the Soviet Union deprived it of access to Soviet technology, since indigenous manufacturers were unable to catch up. Moreover, the PLA's chain of command had been destroyed by the purges and policy shifts of the Cultural Revolution. Training had suffered as well, having been neglected in favor of frenzied political work designed to establish the primacy of the thoughts of Chairman Mao. Allies were sorely needed. It was clear that the only country powerful enough to deter the USSR was the United States which, as it happened, also felt threatened by the expanding might of the Soviet Union. Since the superpower, unlike the later-coming superpower, did not have a long and disputed border with the PRC, it could be considered the less menacing of the two. Negotiations took place, eventually resulting in a rapprochement in 1971 and 1972 and the exchange of formal diplomatic recognition in 1979.

SHAPING THE POST–COLD WAR INTERNATIONAL ORDER

By 1981, the Soviet Union had begun to look less threatening, and the United States less accommodating. Beijing, now led by Deng Xiaoping, eased relations with the former and distanced itself slightly from the latter. The PRC was able to play the United States off against the Soviet Union quite successfully to its own benefit. This strategy worked well until 1989 when a sequence of three events effectively ended this strategy of triangular diplomacy. First, the PRC elite's forcible suppression of peaceful demonstrations at Tiananmen Square and more than a hundred other Chinese cities sharply diminished its image in American public opinion. Television footage of the dead and injured was broadcast repeatedly to horrified audiences, accompanied by emotional commentary on the "butchers of Beijing." President George H. W. Bush, despite his preference for quiet diplomacy, felt compelled to levy sanctions against China. Not surprisingly, the PRC leadership did not react well to this development.

The second event, the disintegration of the Soviet empire, may have been set in train by the first. If the American Revolution was "the shot heard 'round the world," the Tiananmen demonstrations were the tremor preceding the earthquake that shook the communist world. Demonstrations that proved more successful than those in China brought down several Eastern European governments as well as the Berlin Wall, and culminated in the disintegration of the Soviet Union itself in 1991. The USSR splintered into fifteen independent states, thus complicating the Beijing government's ability to practice triangular diplomacy. Moreover, five of the successor states were headed by Muslim governments. Their formation could reinforce separatist movements among the PRC's own traditionally restive Muslim minorities. The same demonstration effect might induce Mongols in China's Inner Mongolian Autonomous Region to try to join Mongolia. Many citizens of the former Mongolian People's Republic, no longer constrained by the atheist propaganda of communism, returned to the practice of lamaist Buddhism. They shared this religion with another traditionally restive part of the PRC, Tibet. Tibet's temporal and spiritual leader, the Dalai Lama, who had been in exile in India since 1959, was invited to visit Mongolia. He was also awarded the Nobel Peace Prize for 1989. These were ominous portents. Globally, the Chinese leadership now faced not two superpowers that it could play off against one another, but a sole superpower that seemed markedly less friendly than before 1989.

A third event was Washington's reaction to Iraq's invasion of Kuwait. President Bush called for a United Nations Security Council resolution authorizing the use of force, and personally called a number of world leaders to lobby for their support. Beijing's leaders, citing the Pancha Sheela's strictures on not violating the territorial integrity of other states and concerned about a possible precedent for a peacekeeping operation directed against China should it attempt to invade Taiwan, were reluctant to consent. Its representatives argued that, while it was wrong for Iraq to invade Kuwait, it would be equally wrong for other nations to invade Iraq—two wrongs do not make a right. But both houses of the U.S. Congress had voted against renewal of the PRC's Most Favored Nation status, and it was within Bush's power to veto this legislation, which was important to China's continued economic growth. In the end, Beijing agreed to abstain in the Security Council vote, thus allowing the peacekeeping operation to proceed. It did not, however, contribute troops to the operation. Chinese leaders were left with the impression that the sole superpower intended to behave like an international bully determined to impose its notions of human rights on the world.

Party and government leaders must have felt beleaguered both internally and internationally. In the four decades since it came to power in 1949, the regime had lost considerable luster with the people it governed. Once supported by the charisma of Mao Zedong's personality, the appeal of communist ideology, and the force of nationalism, the regime now had only the last. As Suisheng Zhao argued in the previous chapter, China's leaders sought to make the most of this asset by appealing to its citizens' patriotism in the face of encroachment by a U.S.-led conspiracy to subvert the government, with strong overtones that this would lead to domestic chaos and economic shortages. Chinese leaders, scholars, and the official media frequently commented on difficulties in post–Soviet Russia and the other successor states, implying that this would be China's fate as well.[2] Official publications reminded citizens of the "century of humiliation" that had been visited on China by Western powers and Japan—the unequal treaties China had been forced to sign, its "enslavement" to Western opium, and the like. Media repeated Mao Zedong's words at the founding of the PRC that "China had stood up,"[3] and urged the youth of the country never to forget.

Internationally, this nationalism took the form of a more assertive foreign policy stance, perhaps to indicate that the PRC would not be bullied. In February 1992, the National People's Congress passed a law unilaterally declaring the PRC's ownership of a number of contested territories, including the Spratly (Nansha), Paracel (Xisha), Senkaku (Diaoyutai) islands and Taiwan. The various claimants to different islands among these include Vietnam, the Philippines, Malaysia, Japan, and Taiwan. The same law claimed for China the right to "adopt all necessary measures to prevent and stop the harmful passage of vessels through its territorial waters" and for "PRC warships or military aircraft to expel the intruders." This caused apprehensions among both claimant and nonclaimant states, the latter category being concerned about the right of free passage for their shipping in these waters. The PRC's subsequent actions indicated that the law had not been passed simply for domestic purposes. In May 1992, for example, Beijing granted oil-exploration rights in a disputed area of the Spratlys to the U.S.-based Crestone Energy Corporation. China also befriended the otherwise isolated Burmese junta, including modernizing port facilities and placing radar installations on Cocos Island that India feared might portend increased PRC naval activity in the Indian Ocean. Nuclear testing continued for some time, despite protests from Japan which, as the only country against whom nuclear weapons have ever been used, has an understandable aversion to them. Japan is also a major aid donor to the PRC.

In the spring of 1995, the Philippine government complained that the PRC had built concrete structures, including radar installations, in another contested area named Mischief Reef. Boundary markers, meant to demarcate the territorial waters claimed by the PRC but located only fifty miles from the Philippines' Palawan Province, had also been discovered. A few weeks after the Philippine revelations, Indonesia announced it had come into possession of a Chinese map showing the Natuna Islands as part of China's exclusive economic zone. Since the Natunas, which contain rich gas deposits, have been under Indonesian jurisdiction, the Jakarta government became quite upset. While both these incidents were smoothed over, the underlying tensions remained. The Indonesian foreign ministry's chief maritime law expert subsequently made several frustrating trips to Beijing to try to clarify the issue. He later complained, "They tell us this is the national heritage of China. . . . They don't argue, they just go on talking about Chinese dynasties. . . .We have a great deal of difficulty analyzing what they're claiming."[4] Several months later, Beijing extended its maritime jurisdiction claim from 370,000 square kilometers off its main coastline to three million square kilometers, which included the disputed Paracel Islands. Indonesian foreign Minister Ali Alatas pointed out that this would be valid only if the PRC were an archipelagic state, which it clearly is not. He expressed the belief that this extended claim might be intended as a precedent for Beijing to claim extended jurisdiction over the also-contested Spratly Islands.[5] Indonesian officials suggested that the PRC was taking an extreme position in order to extract greater concessions than it might otherwise expect to receive. They pointed out that, in addition to calculating baselines as if the PRC were an archipelagic state, China's claims on the Paracels went beyond what the Law of the Sea allowed. Whereas the law stipulates that the ratio of land to sea area within the baselines should not exceed 1:9, China's claim with regard to the Paracels is 1:26.[6]

Beijing also reacted sharply to the visit of President Lee Teng-hui of Taiwan to the United States in June 1995. It had previously warned Washington not to issue Lee a visa, viewing the Taiwan president's statements on eventual unification between Taiwan and the mainland as a cloak for his true, pro-independence, sentiments. Shortly after the visit, the PLA twice bracketed the island with missile tests, disrupting shipping in the busy waterway of the Taiwan Strait and preventing normal fishing activities. It also began several months of war games that looked as if they might be the prelude to an actual invasion. Beijing defended its actions with regard to Taiwan, exclusive economic zones, and the disputed islands as defensive: it was simply defending what rightfully belonged to the People's Republic of China.

A MULTIPOLAR WORLD?

At the same time, Beijing predicted that the bipolar world of the Cold War would be replaced by a multipolar international order. This envisioned a decline in the power of the United States, which would be balanced off by Japan, the European Union, India, Russia, and the PRC itself. To this end, Chinese diplomacy encouraged greater distance between Japan and the United States, pointed out areas of difference between Washington and the states of Europe, and courted good relations with various Middle Eastern and Central Asian states.

Beijing's attempts to form a multilateral coalition against American hegemony while simultaneously threatening one's neighbors produced mixed results. Some policymakers in these neighboring states viewed the PRC as an unstoppable economic juggernaut and felt that placatory policies might achieve more than confrontational ones. This did not necessarily rule out tactics that involved resistance to Chinese expansion, nor efforts to form countervailing coalitions of their own against the PRC. Placatory policies included the regular exchange of visits by heads of state, their cabinet ministers, and members of parliamentary bodies to and from China. Fishing treaties were signed and confidence-building measures discussed. The PRC, along with Japan and South Korea, was given dialogue partner status by the Association of Southeast Asian Nations (ASEAN)[7] and began to explore the feasibility of a free trade agreement between China and ASEAN. China also established close relations with Russia, which soon became its leading supplier of advanced weaponry and an important trading partner. Nor was Beijing's attitude toward the United States overtly hostile: it was China that first approached America with the idea of the strategic partnership discussed in several chapters of this volume. President Clinton appeared to warm to the idea during his second term in office, perhaps believing that the best way to modify the PRC's belligerent behavior was to draw it into a condominium with the United States that would ensure global, or at least regional, stability.

Moves by regional neighbors that involved deterring the PRC from aggression included Indonesia holding in 1996 its largest air, land, and sea military maneuvers in four years. Symbolically, they were held in the Natunas, with foreign military attaches invited (China's attaches declined). Indonesia also ordered F-16 fighter planes from the United States. Beijing did not miss the significance of these moves: a PRC spokesperson complained that Indonesia's attitude could "complicate" the situation in the South China Sea.[8] Malaysia purchased MiG-29 fighter planes from Russia as well as American F/A-18 Hornets. It also constructed a new air force base.[9] Australia began Project Takari, a major fifteen-year upgrade of its armed forces that focused on introducing state-of-the-art equipment for information warfare.[10] Joint naval maneuvers were held between India and Indonesia, and between Malaysia and Indonesia.[11] In December 1995, Indonesia and Australia, two nations whose relationship has historically been characterized by considerable friction, concluded a defense treaty. An Indonesian newspaper noted approvingly that, whereas Australians had until recently thought of Indonesia as the chief threat to their security, they now believed that it "serves as a defense front line for the land of the kangaroos."[12] A few months later, Australia concluded a defense agreement with the United States as well. It included upgrades to the satellite surveillance facility at Pine Gap and a ten-year extension of the American lease to the facility. A joint military exercise involving 17,000 U.S. and Australian personnel, the largest since 1976, was conducted in Queensland in 1997.[13] While no likely adversary was mentioned in the agreement, a respected Australian newspaper editorialized that "the clear logic of maintaining U.S. power in the Asian-Pacific [region] is that it balances the highly unpredictable power of China."[14]

Tokyo's reaction was still more worrisome to the Chinese, who either did not see or did not wish to acknowledge the reasons for Japanese anxieties. The PRC's aggressive actions in the Taiwan Strait in 1995 and 1996 impacted a country that had been Japan's colony from 1895 until the end of World War II; Japanese companies have extensive investments in Taiwan. Should China take over Taiwan, PLA naval patrols, already a concern for Japan, would become still more intrusive. Tokyo approached Washington for an upgrade of the security relationship between the two, which was formalized in the April 1996 "Joint Declaration on Security Alliance For the 21st Century." Citing the existence of instability and uncertainty in the Asia-Pacific Region, the document made specific reference to "heavy concentrations of military force, including nuclear arsenals" [the PRC was the only nuclear power in Asia at that time], "unresolved territorial disputes," and "potential regional conflicts." The two countries agreed to cooperate in "dealing with situations in the areas surrounding Japan which would have an important influence in the peace and security of Japan." Washington promised to maintain its force structure of 100,000 in the region, and Tokyo promised financial assistance to support the force. Beijing demanded Tokyo's assurances that the phrase "areas around Japan" did not include Taiwan. Japanese diplomats replied that they were unable to supply such assurances, since the definition of areas surrounding Japan was situational rather than geographic. This, plus Japan's decision to join American efforts to establish a Theater Missile Defense system, led Beijing to reassess its opinion of the U.S.–Japanese alliance. Whereas heretofore it had seen Washington as mitigating Japanese impulses toward a revival of militarism by including Japan under U.S. military protection, it now saw Washington as fostering the revival of militarism by encouraging Japan to become a partner in its plans to dominate the world, no longer constrained by the counterweight of Soviet power.[15]

India soon joined the list of powers that China was concerned about. In May 1998, Indian defense minister George Fernandes stated that "China is potential threat number one," even greater than that of India's long-term enemy— and PRC ally—Pakistan.[16] Shortly thereafter, India conducted three underground nuclear tests, emphasizing its concerns with rising Chinese power.[17] Pakistan, whose nuclear program was developed with the assistance of the PRC, detonated its own weapons shortly thereafter. Unlike Japan, however, India's anti-China stance was not accompanied by any moves to enhance security cooperation with the U.S. hegemon. The Clinton administration levied sanctions against India and Pakistan for their proliferation activities.

TAMING THE HEGEMON

In the following year, a U.S.-led NATO coalition attacked the Federal Republic of Yugoslavia in order to end the FRY's ethnic cleansing activities in Kosovo. This had still more ominous overtones for the Chinese leadership. In the Persian Gulf scenario of 1991, one sovereign state, Iraq, had conquered another, Kuwait. Moreover, the United Nations Security Council had sanctioned the peacekeeping operation. By contrast, the Kosovo operation involved violating the sovereign rights of a country to do as it wished within its own borders on, as the Chinese saw it, the flimsy excuse that the human rights of a component group thereof were being violated. Moreover, the United Nations had been bypassed. Both could serve as precedents for a U.S. attack on China should it attempt to take Taiwan or the other islands it claims, or even invade the mainland's territory on behalf of the human rights of such groups as Uygurs and Tibetans. Chinese suspicions grew after the American bombing of the Chinese Embassy in Belgrade, as discussed in the previous chapter.

Neither government nor public opinion accepted Washington's explanation that the attack had been accidental. The incident ended the U.S.–China strategic partnership, to the extent that one had ever actually existed. The Kosovo campaign also disabused the Chinese leadership of the notion that the United States was a declining superpower. PRC analysts took note of the improvements in weaponry that had occurred since the Gulf War, and they must also have noted that the multipolar post–Cold War world they had hoped for was rather long in the gestation period.

A commentator in Shanghai's leading newspaper argued that while America vigorously advocated the concept that matters of human rights take precedence over state sovereignty, it would never permit its own sovereignty to be violated by others. This double standard proved that Washington's real aim was to create an arc of encirclement to contain an increasingly strong China.[18] The *China Youth Daily*, for example, ran an article entitled "U.S. Hegemonist Dream," whose author described American history as two centuries of aggressive expansion conditioned by "Protestant 'fatalism,'" meaning, he explained, the belief that god entrusted the Anglo-Saxons with a mission to conquer and Christianize undeveloped nationalities and civilizations. The article concluded that, since the United States has always pursued hegemonism and will continue to do so as long as it is able to maintain its powerful unmatched economic and military strength, "the most effect way of dealing with hegemonism can only be to grow comprehensively powerful ourselves."[19]

The PRC had in fact embarked on a military modernization campaign more than two decades before. Defense budgets had increased by double digit figures each year since 1989, with the actual size of the defense budget believed to be three to four times the reported amount. Still, there was consensus that the needs of economic modernization took precedence over military needs. It would be difficult for China to confront the American military, at least in the immediate future. Analysts pointed out that a major reason for the demise of the Soviet Union was that the Soviets had allowed the United States to inveigle them into an arms buildup that eventually led to the economic collapse of the country. The PRC must not allow itself to be lured into the same trap. Allies were not only useful but crucial in order to break out of this U.S. stranglehold.

Only weeks after the signing of the Japan–U.S. Joint Declaration on Security Alliance for the 21st Century, the leaders of China, Russia, Kazakhstan, Kyrgystan, and Tajikistan met in Shanghai and signed an Agreement on Confidence-Building in the Military Field in the Border Area.[20] The so-called Shanghai Five began to meet regularly in the capitals of member nations. Ties between Moscow and Beijing strengthened, with China regularly referring to Russia as its strategic partner. During President Jiang Zemin's visit to Moscow in 1997, he and then Russian president Boris Yeltsin agreed to promote a new international policy based on multipolarity, and to establish closer trade ties.[21] Border demarcations, troop reductions in border areas, and arms sales were agenda items, as was talk of a "long-term convergence of strategic aims."[22] At a similar meeting in 1999, the two called for the preservation of the 1972 Anti-Ballistic Missile (ABM) Treaty between the United States and the Soviet Union and supported lifting U.N. Security Council sanctions against Iraq.[23] In mid-June 2001, the Shanghai Five welcomed a new member, Uzbekistan, and adopted a new name, the Shanghai Cooperative Organization (SCO). In July, Jiang and Yeltsin's successor, Vladimir Putin, signed a Treaty for Good Neighborliness, Friendship, and Cooperation, the first such agreement between them since the 1950 accord signed by Mao Zedong and Joseph Stalin. The two agreements seemed aimed at a geopolitical realignment allowing Moscow and Beijing to counter Washington's dominance.

Other potential allies were not neglected. There were proposals that the Sino–Russian partnership include Iran[24] (to which the PRC had provided technology and components for weapons of mass destruction[25]) and even, unaccountably in view of the problems between the two, India. Beijing not only argued for ending United Nations sanctions against Iraq, but helped to upgrade Baghdad's air defenses.[26] China continued to aid Burma and other countries on its periphery. A *Wall Street Journal* reporter attributed the large number of PRC aid projects in Cambodia to

> a broader push by Beijing throughout Asia . . . Beijing is forging tight military, political, and economic alliances with most of the dozen countries on its borders. The goal is to redraw geopolitical boundaries and win the regional footholds it has long coveted to project its influence around the region.[27]

POST–SEPTEMBER 11 DEVELOPMENTS

The perception of the leaders of the People's Republic of China is that the nation's geopolitical position has deteriorated since the events of September 11, 2001. Always concerned with being "encircled" by hostile powers, the Beijing leadership has become moreso due to events set in motion by the terrorist attacks on the World Trade Center in New York and the Pentagon. At first, it seemed as if China and the United States might become closer as a result of the attacks. The PRC has acknowledged problems with separatist movements among its indigenous Muslim peoples, some of which have involved bombings and other terrorist activities. A prominent Chinese academic pointed out that his government realized that if the United States could be attacked like this, so could China. Beijing had recently been selected to host the

2008 Olympic Games, and if international terrorism had not been extinguished by then, the country could face a serious threat. He hoped that the newly-found common ground between the two countries could lead to a major improvement in Sino–American relations.[28] Employing a seldom-used hotline that had been set up a few years before, Chinese president Jiang Zemin quickly expressed formal condolences to his counterpart in the White House. The government publicly pledged support for President Bush's call for international support to bring the terrorists to justice. Privately, it asked for understanding of PRC moves against its own ethnic separatist movements and for a reduction in U.S. support for Taiwan's continued separate status. It received neither. Administration spokespersons pointed out that separatist activities were not necessarily terrorist activities, and reiterated long-term U.S. policy that any settlement of the Taiwan issue would have to be achieved by peaceful means.[29] On a personal level, reaction was less supportive. A group of Chinese visiting the United States on the State Department's international visitor program reacted with laughter and evident satisfaction to television footage of the trade center towers falling and the smoldering section of the Pentagon, resulting in their being sent home. Participants in the PRC's chat rooms were sometimes sympathetic, but more often expressed the view that the bullying superpower had got what it deserved.

The Chinese government took several measures that were of assistance to Washington's efforts to deal with the terrorists. It helped to draft and pass resolutions in the United Nations Security Council and General Assembly that condemned the attacks, and supported in principle the coalition attacks on the Taliban government in Afghanistan. The PRC's vote on Resolution 1368 was the first time that it voted in favor of authorizing the international use of force.[30] Beijing did not object to its longtime ally, Pakistan, cooperating with Washington against the terrorists, sealed its border with Afghanistan, and promised to share intelligence that might lead to apprehension of the terrorists with the United States.

However, analysts who predicted a new dawn in Sino–American relations were soon disabused of the notion, as geopolitical realities took precedence over thoughts that there could be a united front against terrorism. Beijing very quickly began to interpret the American response to the September 11 events in light of its post–Cold War world view of a hegemonistic United States bent on imposing its vision of the ideal global order on all other states. The rhetoric of China-as-historical-victim was revived. For example, in an article discussing the importance of national defense education in China, the country's defense minister gave prominence to what he claimed were nearly 1,000 unequal treaties that China had had to sign during a century of humiliation, being "oppressed and exploited, subjected to unprecedented disaster and humiliation."[31] "We must not," he cautioned, "forget this bitter historical experience."

Not humiliation but frustration must have been Beijing's reaction as the Shanghai Cooperative Organization faded to irrelevancy by post–September 11 developments, thus diminishing the effects of years of Chinese efforts to avoid encirclement on its northern and Central Asian borders. SCO members offered various degrees of bilateral support to the American campaign to root out terrorism, including basing rights in Tajikistan and Uzbekistan. Uzbekistan failed to send a representative to the May 2002 meeting of the SCO, and those members who attended were unable to agree on concrete steps to boost military cooperation among them.[32] Beijing became concerned that the U.S. presence in Central Asia might become permanent, to the detriment of the PRC's own interests there. Russia also moved closer to the United States after September 11. President Vladimir Putin quickly agreed to allow U.S. troops to be deployed in Central Asia and the Caucasus. By 2002, he had acquiesced gracefully in America's withdrawal from the ABM Treaty, which the Chinese had worked hard to oppose. In May 2002, Bush and Putin signed a treaty committing their countries to reduce their nuclear warheads from about 6,000 apiece to no more than 2,200 by the end of 2012, issued a joint declaration on the establishment of a new strategic relationship between them, and joined with the countries of the North Atlantic Treaty Organization (NATO) to issue the Rome Declaration. Russia would have equal status with the nineteen members of an alliance whose original raison d'être was containment of the Soviet Union.[33]

Chinese analysts assessed the meeting as signifying "the complete assimilation of Russia into the American orbit."[34] In the words of a leading Chinese authority on international affairs, Russia had put a final end to its confrontation with the United States and NATO, becoming the latter's ally rather than its enemy. He opined that, while it was still too early to say that Russia was integrated into the West, Russia's westward tilt had definitely "upset the balance between hegemonistic and anti-hegemonistic forces in the world."[35]

The PRC was also unhappy with America's efforts to widen the war against terrorism to Southeast Asian states where movements and or cells were believed to be operating. The arrival of U.S. military advisors in the Philippines to help counter Muslim insurgents and American claims that certain Indonesian groups such as the Laskar Jihad were harboring Al Qaeda operatives were interpreted as Washington using the events of September 11 as an excuse to spread its tentacles further around the world.[36]

Beijing also looked with dismay on a warming trend in U.S.–Indian relations after September 11. In January 2002, Indian Defense Minister Fernandes (the same individual who declared China public enemy number one at the time India carried out its 1998 nuclear tests) paid a week-long visit to Washington that resulted in several agreements on military cooperation.[37] Two months later, Indian prime minister Atal Behari Vajpayee addressed the U.S.

Congress, declaring that the two countries were "natural allies;"[38] Commander-in-Chief of the U.S. Pacific Command, Admiral Dennis Blair, added that military cooperation with India had reached "unprecedented levels." A *Renmin Wang* reporter commented thus on an exercise involving the Indian and American navies:

> The United States understands the important military position and strength of India in the region. Though it is a superpower, it has too many enemies and there are bound to be some places that it cannot attend to. So why not let India help lighten the burden? India, on the other hand, can raise the banner of antiterrorism to use as a pretext to gradually achieve its strategic objectives and make it difficult for countries in the Asia-Pacific region to find a reason to oppose its actions. Therefore, the two sides are simply too happy to cooperate.[39]

A Taiwan newspaper reported that Taipei now has military ties with India as well.[40]

Japan also continued what Beijing considered its slide toward militarism in alliance with the United States again, according to Chinese analysis, using the pretext of shoring up its defenses against terrorism. Larger and wealthier than most of the PRC's neighbors, Japan is less likely to feel a need to accommodate its behavior to Beijing's demands. Its cabinet ministers courted China's anger through such actions as visiting the Yasukuni Shrine—where those who made war on China are among the honorees—discussing cuts in Japan's overseas development aid to the PRC,[41] and hinting that Japan might seek to acquire nuclear weapons.[42] In Japan, ill feelings were exacerbated when Chinese police entered the grounds of the Japanese consulate in Shenyang to drag off asylum-seeking North Koreans.[43] Japanese Prime Minister Koizumi visited Canberra in May 2002, discussing ties among his country, Australia, and the United States. According to the Singapore-based *Straits Times*, "a major defense relationship, probably directed against China, is taking shape . . . in the form of a triangle."[44]

Sensing that the post–September 11 trend had worsened its position, Beijing made efforts to shore up its diplomacy. The PRC was an active participant at the ASEM (Asia–Europe Meeting) held in Copenhagen in 2002 and described as "a forum to balance U.S. power . . . these two parts of the world need each other not only to face up to an eventual 'pax americana' but also for a host of other reasons."[45] At the 2002 meeting of the ASEAN Regional Forum, of which China is a dialogue partner, the PRC tabled a security plan that members interpreted as a challenge to the United States.[46] Though not extraordinary at first glance, the plan's emphasis on enhancing trust through dialogue and promoting security through cooperation on the basis of the Five Principles of the People and other "universally recognized norms governing international relations"[47] played on misgivings in several nations about the U.S. policy on preemptive strikes on territories believed to harbor terrorists.

Beijing also continues to use its growing economic power to further its diplomatic ends. In September 2002, the China National Offshore Oil Corporation (CNOOC) signed an $8.5 billion deal with Indonesia's state-owned oil and gas company, Pertamina, to develop a large natural gas field.[48] In the same month, China agreed with ASEAN to form a free trade framework, with the contracting parties stating their intention to begin cutting tariffs on certain products by the end of 2004.[49] Also in September, Beijing, in what was interpreted as raising the country's diplomatic profile in the Middle East, named an experienced former ambassador to several Arab states as its special envoy to the area.[50] The PRC continued to purchase arms from Russia, and conducted military maneuvers with several Central Asian states.[51] In reviewing President Jiang Zemin's spring 2002 visit to five countries, a Hong Kong magazine speculated that the inclusion of Libya and Iran in his itinerary indicated that the PRC intended to join forces with "axis of evil" states in order to counter America's global dominance.[52]

Two members of the prestigious Chinese Academy of Social Sciences attempted to counter the argument that the PRC was becoming aggressive, arguing that a more self-confident China would be a more responsible member of the world community. Nations conduct diplomacy based on both their self-images and images of the outside world, and since the PRC no longer viewed itself as a county on the edge of collapse but as a rising power with increasing capability to shape its environment, it would behave responsibly on the world scene. Beijing, they predicted, would neither try to reclaim lost territories nor seize the whole of the South China Sea, and it would "not try to re-establish the '*Zhonghua* [China] Order'[53] by bullying regional states into submission." With Chinese companies like Sinopec and PetroChina increasingly behaving like British Petroleum or Shell, there was no need for the PRC to satisfy its energy needs through conquest. And, while the United States would remain one of the focal points of Beijing's security calculus, its "great power foreign relations" (*daguo waijiao*) had moved away from being America-centric to putting more emphasis on interactions with other powers.[54]

CONCLUSION

With its ability to practice triangular diplomacy constrained by the disintegration of the Soviet Union, Chinese diplomacy attempted to provide for the security of the state by forming countervailing coalitions with other states, including the successor states of the Soviet Union, Europe, Southeast Asia, and, to some extent, Japan. Analysts predicted the emergence of a multipolar world, with the United States declining in power as other states or groups thereof assumed greater importance. The U.S. economic performance remained strong throughout the 1990s, however, and the U.S.–NATO performance in Kosovo indicated a superpower that not only was not in decline but, from the Chinese point of view, was becoming more aggressive. The U.S. response to the September 11, 2001 attacks on its territory included drawing closer to several of the centers of power that PRC diplomacy had hoped would function either independently or in concert with the PRC. Chinese sources interpreted Washington's invasion of Iraq as an illegal war undertaken to establish a new international energy order under American control. It saw this, and not a regime change in Baghdad or the dismantling of weapons of mass destruction, as America's primary motive.[55]

While these were not trends that the PRC perceived as positive, they could prove ephemeral. Should the U.S. economy weaken markedly, or should Washington handle the Iraq problem in such a way as to antagonize large numbers of other states, for example, the trend could reverse. Chinese diplomacy continues to court states on behalf of its preferred world order, as well as to pursue amicable relations with the United States, notwithstanding its view of the United States as a hegemonistic superpower.

NOTES

1. All of the PRC's ambassadors were recalled save the one accredited to Egypt; a charge d'affairs remained in India. Red Guards sacked their own country's foreign ministry in Beijing, and also invaded the British embassy, killing one of its personnel.

2. Christopher Marsh, "Learning From Your Comrade's Mistakes: The Impact of the Soviet Past on China's Future," *Communist and Post-Communist Studies* 35 (September 2003).

3. Recently, doubts have surfaced that Mao actually said this at Tiananmen Square on October 1, 1949. He has, however, been credited with doing so for several decades. When Chen Shui-bian was inaugurated as president of the Republic of China on Taiwan in May 2000, his speech consciously paralleled Mao's alleged words by announcing that "Taiwan has stood up."

4. Ambassador Hashim Djalal, quoted in John McBeth, "Oil-Rich Diet: Beijing Is Being Asked to Explain Its Maritime Appetite," *Far Eastern Economic Review*, 27 April 1995, 28.

5. Rizal Sukma. "Indonesia Toughens China Stance," *Far Eastern Economic Review*, 5 September 1996, 28.

6. John McBeth, "Exercising Sovereignty: Indonesia Sends A Message from Natuna," *Far Eastern Economic Review*, 19 September 1996, 17.

7. <www.aseansec.org> (14 April 2003). See "External Relations" section.

8. McBeth, "Exercising Sovereignty," 17.

9. "Completion of New Air Force Base Expected in December," *New Straits Times* (Kuala Lumpur), 5 June 1996, 9.

10. John Stackhouse, "Australia Learns Vital Lesson From Gulf War," *The Australian Financial Review* (Sydney), 2 July 1996, 49.

11. McBeth, "Exercising Sovereignty," 17.

12. Ferdinandus R. Sius, "The Significance of the Republic of Indonesia–Australia Security Agreement," *Suara Perbaruan* (Jakarta), 10 January 1996, 2–3.

13. Craig Skehan, "Pine Gap Improvements, Exercises with U.S.," *The Sydney Morning Herald,* 29 July 1996.

14. "Security Links With the U.S.," *The Australian Financial Review*, 29 July 1996.

15. Patrick Tyler, "China Cautions U.S. and Japan On Security Pact," *New York Times*, 18 April 1996, A5.

16. *Agence France Presse* (New Delhi), "Beijing Number One Threat, Says India Official," in *South China Morning Post* (Hong Kong), 4 May 1998.

17. Abhijit Dutta, "India Simply Had To Do It," *The Statesman* (Calcutta), May 20, 1998 <www.thestatesman.net>; C. Raja Mohan, *The Hindu* (New Delhi), 18 May 1998, <www.hinduonline.com>.

18. Pan Rui, "Take A Further Look At the Dual Character of U.S. Policy Toward China," *Jiefang Ribao* (Liberation Daily), Shanghai, 22 May 1999, 7, translated in FBIS CPP 19990630000628.

19. Lan Wenxuan, "U.S. Hegemonist Dream," *Zhongguo Qingnian Bao* (China Youth News), Beijing, 24 May 1999, 2, translated in FBIS CPP 199900626000623.

20. Commentary, "Historic Partnership," *China Daily* (Beijing), 27 April 1996, 3.

21. James Harding and Chrystia Freeland, "In Search of a Multipolar World," *Financial Times* (London), 8 November 1997, 4.

22. "Arms Key Issue as Sino–Russian Embrace Tightens," *South China Morning Post*, 26 April 1997, <www.scmp.com>; "Can a Bear Love a Dragon?" *The Economist* (London), 26 April 1997, 19–20; 22.

23. Michael Laris, "In China, Yeltsin Lashes Out At Clinton, Criticisms of Chechen War Are Met With Blunt Reminder of Russian Nuclear Power," *Washington Post*, 10 December 1999, A35.

24. "Rafsanjani, Li: Economic and Political Cooperation To Satisfy Needs," *Associated Press*, 5 May 1997.

25. See, e.g., U.S. China Security Review Commission, *Report to Congress: The National Security Implications of the Economic Relationship Between the United States and China*, Washington, D.C. July 2002, 135.

26. "China Sidesteps Claims Of Aiding Iraqi Air Defenses," *Associated Press* (Beijing), 20 February 2001.

27. Karby Leggett, "China Forges Alliances in Effort To Gain More Influence in Asia," *Wall Street Journal*, 7 June, 2001 (Internet).

28. Erik Eckholm, "China's About Face: Support For U.S. On Terror," *New York Times*, 30 September 2001, I: 6.

29. A year after the attacks, the Bush administration added the heretofore obscure East Turkistan Independence Movement (ETIM) to its list of international terrorist organiza-

tions. Those familiar with the group denied that ETIM used terrorist techniques; there was much speculation that the administration wanted to appease Beijing in order to soften its opposition to U.S. plans to invade Iraq. See, e.g., Erik Eckholm, "U.S. Labeling of Group in China As Terrorist Is Criticized," *New York Times*, 13 September 2002, 1.

30. Philip Pan, "For Bush and Jiang, Questions of Risk and Reward," *Washington Post*, 18 October 2001, A26.

31. Chi Haotian, "Take Reinforcement of National Defense Education as Basic Project For Fortifying and Prospering Country," Beijing, Xinhua, 19 September 2002, in FBIS CPP 20020919000035.

32. Willy Wo-Lap Lam, "'Beijing's NATO' Hits Stumbling Block," CNN, 16 May 2002, <www.cnn.com>.

33. David Sanger, "Bush and Putin Sign Pact for Steep Nuclear Arms Cuts," *New York Times*, 25 May 2002, A1; A7; Ian Black, "Russia and NATO Greet Arrival of a Warm Front: Vladimir Putin and Western Leaders Consign the Cold War To History at a Round-Table Summit in Italy," *The Guardian* (London), 29 May 2002, 13.

34. Ching Cheong, "U.S.–Russia Summit Worries China," *Straits Times*, 31 May 2002, <www.straitstimes.com>.

35. Zhou Shuchun, "September 11th Accelerates Change Of World Order, Intensifies U.S. Unilateralism and Russian Tilt to West," *Liaowang*, no. 23, 3 June 2002, 10–13, CPP 20020611000046.

36. Heru Andriyanto and Zhai Jingsheng, "Disputes on Anti-Terrorism Straiten Indonesia–U.S. Ties," *Xinhua*, 20 September 2002, <www.xinhuanet.com/english/index.htm>.

37. "India to Bolster Military Ties with U.S.," *Reuters* (New Delhi), 15 January 2002. In May 2002, the U.S.–India Defense Policy Group issued a summary of the results of their coordination thus far, including combined naval patrols in the Strait of Malacca; resumption of defense trade, beginning with the sale of Firefinder radars to India; combined special forces airborned exercises in Agra; holding a U.S.–India Ballistic Missile Defense workshop in Colorado Springs, and signing a General Security of Military Information Agreement to facilitate the exchange of defense technology. <http://www/defenselink.mil/news/May2002/b05232002/bt267-02.html> (25 May 2002).

38. Chandrashekhar Dasgupta, "Partnerships On Specific Issues Will Boost India–U.S. Relations," *The Telegraph* (Calcutta), 23 April 2002, 12.

39. Qian Feng, "India Wants To Be 'The International Maritime Police' of the Malacca Strait," *Renmin Wang*, 20 April 2002, in CPP 200220420000026.

40. "Taipei 'Fostering Military Ties With India,'" *South China Morning Post*, 3 January 2002, quoting *Lienho Pao* (*United Daily News*), Taipei.

41. John Pomfret, "Japan Likely To Cut Aid To China: Economic, Military Rivalries Pushing Two Nations Apart" *Washington Post*, 10 September 2002, A11.

42. "Beijing Shocked By Japan's Nuclear Remark," *Reuters*, 3 June 2002; Howard W. French, "Taboo against Nuclear Arms Is Being Challenged in Japan," *New York Times*, 9 June 2002, I1; I4.

43. "Asylum-Seeker Policy Needed," *Yomiuri Shimbun* (Tokyo), 23 May 2002, <www.yomiuri.co.jp>.

44. "Aussies Plan Defense Triangle with Japan, U.S.," *Straits Times*, 3 May 2002 <www.straitstimes.com>.

45. Eric Teo, "ASEM: A Forum to Balance U.S. Power," *Straits Times*, 2 October 2002, <www.straitstimes.com>.

46. Kavi Chongkittavorn, "China Challenges U.S. with New Security Ideas," *The Nation* (Bangkok), 12 August 2002.

47. *Xinhua* (Bandar Seri Bagawan), "China Releases Position Paper, Offers New Security Concept At ASEAN," 1 August 2002.

48. Matthew Jones and Tom McCawley, "Pertamina Signs $8.5 Billion Deal with China," *Financial Times* (London), 27 September 2002, 29.

49. Laila Rahman and Azlan Othman, "ASEAN, China Agree to Start Free Trade Framework," *Borneo Bulletin* (Bandar Seri Begawan), 14 September 2002, <http://www.brunei-online.com/bb/>.

50. Daniel Kwan, "Mideast Role Limited, Say Experts," *South China Morning Post*, 26 September 2002, <www.scmp.com>.

51. "China and Kyrgyzstan Plan Joint Exercises," *Straits Times*, 17 September 2002, <www.straitstimes.com>.

52. Ch'ang Ch'ing, "Communist China Played the Good-Guy–Bad-Guy Game in Diplomacy," *Cheng Ming* (Hong Kong), no. 295, 1 May 2002, 34–36, in CPP 20020502000039.

53. Chinese and English are in original text.

54. Zhang Yunlin, and Tang Shiping, "More Self-Confident China Will Be a Responsible Power," *Straits Times*, 2 October 2002, <www.straitstimes.com>.

55. See, for example, Liao Lei, "Dispatching Troops Without a Just Cause Will Involve Endless Trouble," *Xinhua* (Beijing), 27 March 2003, and Feng Yujun, "International Oil Strategy Faces a Card-Shuffling," *Renmin Ribao* (Beijing), 10 April 2003, 13.

Opportunities and Challenges
for U.S.–China Relations

J. Stapleton Roy

As the world enters the twenty-first century, America's relations with China are important for several reasons. First, the degree of cooperation between China and the United States has a direct impact on the war against terrorism and on the freedom of action that we have in dealing with problem regimes in Iraq, North Korea, and other parts of the world. Secondly, China is a permanent member of the United Nations Security Council, on which it has veto power, and it is a vast country that has a great deal of influence around the world. Finally, there is another, perhaps more important reason. We Americans are quite naturally focused on the issue of terrorism, but the emergence of China as a stronger and more prosperous country, a process that has occurred with unprecedented speed over the last twenty years, has far greater significance than the issue of terrorism for the future of peace and stability in East Asia, and indeed for the world as a whole.

As Andrew Nathan discusses in a preceding chapter, China is in the midst of the most important leadership transition in recent memory. Over the course of a few months, beginning with the party congress in November 2002 and ending with the National People's Congress the following spring, China gained a new head of the Communist Party and a new premier of the State Council, the top party and government leadership positions. In both cases, the replacements brought in members of China's fourth generation of leaders, a group considerably younger than the retiring third generation headed by Jiang Zemin. One does not get to be a successor in China without being seen as a reliable implementer of existing policy, but a generational change cannot occur without bringing in people who think differently. Anyone with children will immediately recognize that nurturing someone to think exactly as you do in your own home does not work. Children always think differently from the way their parents do, and part of this phenomenon has to do with generational difference. It would thus be foolish to think that China's new generation of leaders is going to be simply a carbon copy of the current generation.

This leadership transition is significant for another reason, however. This is the first time that China's top communist party leader has been replaced through a normal political process. All of Mao Zedong's successors as CCP general secretary had been purged. For a peaceful leadership transition in China to occur is significant in itself. But it will also be important for the United States to position itself so that when the new generation of leaders emerges in China, they do not begin with a sense of encroachment and dangerous nationalism in looking at the United States, issues probed by June Teufel Dreyer and Suisheng Zhao elsewhere in this volume. Rather, the outlook for U.S.–China relations will be much improved if China's fourth generation of leaders see the United States as a country with which they can cooperate.

Fortunately, for the moment U.S.–China relations are relatively stable and cooperative. As Strobe Talbott pointed out in chapter 1, however, it was not that long ago that this administration's rhetoric referred to China as our strategic competitor. Nor has it been long since the United States and China came uncomfortably close to confrontation over the EP-3 incident of April 2001. The important thing to remember, however, is that the Bush Administration was already seeking to develop a more normal relationship with China well before September 11, 2001. This was reflected in June 2001 testimony to Congress by Assistant Secretary of State James Kelly, and demonstrated again when the United States was able to reach final agreement on China's terms for entry into the World Trade Organization before September 11. There is no question, of course, that September 11 had an enormous impact on the U.S. view of relations with China. Suddenly the U.S. focus on the terrorist threat made it imperative for us to give priority to cooperation with a government like China's, if at all possible, in order to pursue more effectively the war against terrorism. Fortunately, and this was not an accidental decision on Beijing's part, China facilitated such cooperation by its quick and positive response to the September 11 attacks.

At the moment, therefore, relations between the United States and China are relatively smooth. China is now a member of the WTO, which has stimulated enormous interest in our business community in trade and investment opportunities in China. Moreover, China's economy continues to be one of the fastest growing economies in the world. Nevertheless, while there are myriad reasons why we should use this opportunity to try to stabilize our relationship with China, there are lurking problems in the U.S.–China relationship that we would be foolish to ignore.

First, Americans have widely divergent views of China. It was no accident that during the 2000 presidential campaign advisors to Governor Bush talked about China as a strategic competitor. Even now it is easy to find articles and speakers explaining why a stronger China is going to be more threatening to the United States. On the other hand, one can also find people who think that China has been moving in the right direction over the last twenty years. As some of the contributors to this volume argue in preceding chapters, China today is a more open country, and power is more institutionalized. Additionally, as Minxin Pei discussed, Chinese students are flooding our country. China today has officials at all levels of government who have been educated in American universities.

None of this existed twenty years ago. Not surprisingly, many people see this as a positive evolution. However, if one looks at the way China is sometimes discussed by U.S. government officials, it is often not clear which China it is that they are talking about: the China that has abandoned the rigid ideology of the past, that sees its interests as closely linked to the industrialized countries of the West, and that is successfully implementing market-based economic development; or the China that is growing stronger and potentially more threatening, and that is preparing for military conflict with the United States.

The second problem is the challenge posed to America by the modernization of China's military. And finally, there is the very troublesome issue of Taiwan, which is getting worse, not better. It is a problem that, if mishandled, poses a genuine risk of military conflict between the United States and China. Such a conflict would have an enormous impact not only on both countries, but on the world as a whole. In the pages that follow, I will consider each of these issues and hopefully shed some light on the situation as I see it.

AMERICA VIEWS THE MIDDLE KINGDOM

Ambivalence about China is not restricted to the United States; one can find it throughout Asia. Understandably, China's neighbors are worried about China's growing power, but at the same time they see incredible opportunities in China's rapidly developing economy, leading them to seek to cooperate with China, not contain it. This is also true for Japan. While Japan historically has been a rival of China, there is now enormous interest on the part of Japanese in cooperating with China. The low cost of labor in China has led to the phenomenon referred to as the "hollowing out" of industry in Northeast Asia, where the manufacturing industries of Japan, Korea, and Taiwan are being transferred to the mainland to take advantage of the economic opportunities there to improve production efficiency. We are not alone, therefore, in our ambivalence about China. In our case, however, it is particularly strong because it includes a military component. Many Americans sense that perhaps we are indeed China's competitor in this way.

This duality in our perception of China is reflected in the way Americans talk about China. For example, shortly before the October 2002 Crawford Summit, Secretary of State Colin Powell gave an interview in which he was quoted as saying, "we see China as a friend now. No one in the administration sees China as an enemy."[1] Not long before that, our Ambassador to Beijing, Ambassador Randt, was quoted as saying, "China is one of America's strongest allies in the war against terrorism." He went on to express confidence that China would support U.S.-led action against Iraq now that President Bush had taken his case to the United Nations.[2] He hastened to add, however, that there was no "devil's compact." In his estimate, cooperation against terrorism did not mean that China was going to receive a free pass with respect to issues such as nonproliferation, human rights, religious freedom, or Taiwan.

In contrast to these positive assessments, the Congressionally-mandated U.S.–China Security Review Commission had issued a report in the summer of 2002 that was highly skeptical of our relationship with Beijing.[3] It concluded that U.S. policies toward China have been disjointed and not necessarily based on a uniform view of what is in our national interest. It claimed that there were also important areas in which China's policies ran directly counter to U.S. national security interests. In other words, at a time when the administration was trying to improve relations with China, a commission set up by Congress was arguing that we were dealing with China in ways that were undermining our own security. In an area of particular importance to the business community, the Commission contended that current U.S. policies had failed adequately to monitor the transfer of economic resources and security-related technologies to China. The implicit message was that American business people were lax in letting dangerous technologies and profits go to China.

While this Commission was a not an official part of the U.S. government, similar skepticism about China was contained in President Bush's first National Security Strategy for the United States that was issued in September 2002. In it, the president called our relationship with China an important part of our strategy to promote a stable, peaceful, and prosperous Asia-Pacific region. On the positive side, he welcomed the emergence of a strong, peaceful, and prosperous China, and he affirmed that the United States "seeks a constructive relationship with a changing China." At the same time, the strategy statement contended that in "pursuing advanced military capabilities that can threaten its neighbors in the Asia–Pacific region, China is following an outdated path that in the end will hamper its own pursuit of national greatness." Instead of making the case that cooperative relations with China could make a stronger China less dangerous, these statements did not present a clear strategy for dealing with China. Americans were left with the impression that while we want a good cooperative relationship with Beijing, China is a dangerous country, and we must really watch our backs in dealing with it.

Finally, consider the Pentagon's *Annual Report on the Military Power of the People's Republic of China*.[4] The most recent iteration thereof concluded that preparing for a potential conflict in the Taiwan Strait was the primary driver of China's military modernization and that China's goal is to complicate intervention by the United States in a Taiwan Strait crisis. One does not have to be a military strategist to interpret that language as saying that China is preparing for war with the United States.

It is easy to see why Americans are confused about China. Instead of giving us an integrated view of China and a sense of how to integrate China's positive and negative aspects into a policy approach that will make a stronger and more prosperous China less threatening to U.S. interests, we are presented with two Chinas: the dangerous China that we have to stay away from and that we must keep our businessmen from trading with; and the cooperative China, whose support we need on terrorism and other things.

June Teufel Dreyer's contribution to this volume, which discusses America's encroachment upon China, is particularly illuminating because it gives one a sense of how Chinese feel about other countries who are dealing with them, particularly powerful states that in their eyes are encroaching on the Middle Kingdom. To gain perspective, it might be helpful for us Americans to step back from time to time and think about our role in the world. After all, it is we who have the biggest defense budget in the world; it is we who are increasing our military spending faster than other countries. Do other countries see us as aggressive and threatening because we are building up our military? The answer is that some do and some do not. Expanded defense budgets are not inherently threatening; how they are seen depends on how countries perceive each others actions and intentions.

DEFENDING THE MIDDLE KINGDOM

In looking at the factors that affect Chinese military spending, the first thing to bear in mind is that China was a lot less smart than the United States in selecting its geographic location. China is surrounded by powerful neighbors, none of which is a natural ally. In my own lifetime, China has been in armed conflict with Japan, the United States, Korea, India, the Soviet Union, and

Vietnam. If I were to provide a list of six countries that it would be advisable not to get into armed conflict with, that would be the list. But China has fought all of them, and only in the case of the Soviet Union was it a relatively minor conflict.

As June Teufel Dreyer pointed out in the previous chapter, for the last decade since the Gulf War China's defense spending has indeed been rising, but this followed a two-decade period when China starved its military. During the 1980s, it essentially put the bulk of its resources into economic development. During the 1970s, due to the fact that the head of China's military had allegedly been the leader of a failed coup attempt against Mao Zedong, China's leaders were trying to reduce the military's influence in national affairs, and the defense budget was modest. Only after China's economic reforms had begun to produce rapid growth did China's defense spending begin to rise. Last year, China's defense budget increased by 17 percent. In terms of its official budget, that brings the sum to $17 billion dollars; which is barely the cost of a couple of B-2 bombers. Experts estimate that China's actual defense spending may be three to five times higher, because not all allocations to the military are reflected in the official defense budget. That would raise China's defense spending to the level of Japan's, but China's defense needs are enormously greater than Japan's, which is under the U.S. nuclear umbrella. China has lengthy land borders and is surrounded by powerful countries.

So what is the proper level for China's defense spending? The first thing to consider is that much of Chinese military equipment is obsolete. China's military leaders certainly want to modernize their military. The question is whether this reflects an intention to engage in aggression their neighbors? Perhaps, but there might be other reasons as well, such as to defend the country more aggressively. Every country in the world, and China in particular, was deeply affected by the Gulf War in 1991. They also saw the pictures of laser-guided bombs going down smokestacks, followed by the use of air power against Kosovo in the Balkans. These demonstrations of the use of modern military equipment were particularly troubling for a country like China that has relied upon the strategy of "people's war." This strategy derived from China's military weakness, which meant it could not keep foreign countries from fighting a war on Chinese territory. China, therefore, was the only country in the world with missiles targeted on itself, so that missiles could be launched to destroy the enemy on Chinese territory. The use of modern military technology thus clearly illustrated to China that the strategy of people's war was obsolescent and it was imperative to modernize its military.

Additionally, there are problems in the Taiwan Strait, where the military confrontation has grown more intense since the mid-1990s. The Chinese military is using this as a justification for building up its military spending. It is this buildup that was the focus of the comments in the U.S. Defense Department report referred to earlier. There is some basis for that buildup. China has territorial disputes with Japan and various Southeast Asian countries over islands in the East and South China Seas. The United States is moving ahead with a missile defense program that has the potential, if expanded beyond current plans, to negate China's strategic deterrent. This could cause China to build up its own strategic missile capability so that it would retain the ability to retaliate against the United States.

There are thus numerous reasons why China would want to increase its military spending that are not linked to aggressive intentions on the part of China against its neighbors. And yet, when we talk about Chinese defense spending, we almost never talk about the context in which Chinese defense spending takes place. What does it mean for China to increase its defense budget by 17 percent per year if one does not consider what Japan, the United States, and Russia are doing? All of this is relevant if we wish to analyze the situation intelligently. The fact that we do not integrate the necessary information into our analysis of China means that it is hard to have a sense as to whether China is a threat or whether it is behaving normally. It is also true, of course, that if we were to draw down our significant military presence in East Asia, China's military buildup would be potentially more threatening.

TAIWAN AND THE U.S.–CHINA RELATIONSHIP

As noted in the beginning of this chapter, our relationship with China is in pretty decent shape. Jiang Zemin's visit to the Crawford ranch and the important talks he held with President Bush are part of the larger process of improving ties between the United States and China that became strained after the EP-3 incident in the spring of 2001. A lingering problem, however, relates to the Taiwan issue, which is the most troublesome issue in our relationship with China, and which has been a central concern to both sides since we normalized relations in the 1970s. Our relations with China and Taiwan are still based upon the three communiqués negotiated over twenty years ago (See appendix 1) and the Taiwan Relations Act. While the world has changed, this framework has not, and it is no longer as effective as it once was in containing problem areas.

The first communiqué, the Shanghai Communiqué, negotiated in 1972, established the principle of one China as the basis for our relationship with Beijing. At the time, the government of the Republic of China on Taiwan claimed to be the government of all of China. The one China principle was thus vital to it as well. Its rule on Taiwan was justified by its claim that as the government of all of China, it was a legitimate government for Taiwan. As a government that could not have national elections to legitimize its rule, it depended on the one China principle to support its right to be the legal government of Taiwan. We, of course, at the time recognized the Republic of China as the government of all of China. Under the one China principle, however, we could only recognize one Chinese government at a time as the government of all of China.

This situation has now changed. Today there is democracy in Taiwan, and elections are held for the government there. The one China principle is no longer needed to establish the legitimacy of the government. Not surprisingly, given these changed circumstances, the two sides of the Taiwan Strait have since 1992 been unable to agree on a common definition of one China. The two sides were able to start a political dialogue across the Strait at the beginning of the 1990s, but since then they have not been able to continue the dialogue because of differences over the one China principle. The Shanghai Communiqué thus does not play the same role anymore.

The second communiqué is the normalization communiqué, which was issued in December 1978 just as the United States was about to establish diplomatic relations with Beijing. In this communiqué, the U.S. government accepted the principle of unofficiality as the basis for our continuing relations with Taiwan. It was difficult to do this, and in April 1979, the U.S. Congress passed the Taiwan Relations Act to make it possible for our agreements with Taiwan, which had been agreements with a sovereign government, to continue in effect even though we no longer recognized Taiwan as a sovereign government. This Act also provided for a special U.S. office in Taiwan that would by staffed by U.S. government employees who had officially left their government positions. The American Institute in Taiwan, is thus an unofficial organization, even though it is, in effect, a surrogate embassy there. This arrangement was a subterfuge, but it is an open subterfuge designed to be consistent with the principle of unofficiality in our dealing with Taiwan.

A lot has changed since then. Today, the U.S. government sends cabinet members to Taiwan. Can a cabinet member be unofficial? In the spring of 2002, Taiwan's defense minister traveled to Florida, and the U.S. Deputy Secretary of Defense met with him there. They did not meet in the Pentagon, but does the fact that President Jiang Zemin and President Bush met in Crawford mean that such a meeting was unofficial? Does this mean that the United States is in compliance with the normalization communiqué? The official U.S. government position is, of course, that we are, but the Chinese do not see it that way.

Finally, the third communiqué, the August 17, 1982 Communiqué, dealt with the issue of U.S. arms sales to Taiwan that could not be solved in earlier negotiations. In establishing diplomatic relations with Beijing, the United States ended its defense treaty with Taiwan, removed its military presence from Taiwan, and broke diplomatic relations with the Republic of China, but the United States insisted on the right to continue selling arms to Taiwan to meet its defensive needs, and to ensure it could not be coerced by the mainland. In the 1982 Communiqué, however, the U.S. government agreed gradually to decrease the level of our arms sales to Taiwan, while Beijing committed itself to seeking reunification by peaceful means as its fundamental policy.

This communiqué was undermined by subsequent developments. In 1992 the United States decided to sell F-16 fighter jets to Taiwan, which China viewed as a violation of the understandings in the 1982 Communiqué. Three years later, China began to threaten the use of force against Taiwan if Taiwan tried to become independent. This reflected Chinese dissatisfaction with the reversal of U.S. assurances to Beijing that Taiwan President Lee Teng-hui would not be permitted to make an unofficial visit to the United States in 1995. These threats by Beijing provided the United States with all the more reason to sell more arms to Taiwan. So while the 1982 Communiqué is still there as a paper document, it is not serving its original purpose of helping to stabilize the U.S.–China relationship.

Another potential problem relates to efforts in Congress to insert language into the National Defense Authorization Act calling for closer cooperation between the U.S. Defense Department and Taiwan, even to the extent of having interoperability between our military forces.[5] Beijing views these efforts as a step toward resuming a formal U.S. defense relationship with Taiwan.

Fortunately, although we have not been able to solve these problems, we have been able to keep them from blocking cooperation between China and the United States. For example, the meetings at the October 2002 Crawford Summit were successfully used to improve mutual understanding between the two sides.

THE FUTURE OF CHINA AND U.S.–CHINA RELATIONS

China's period of extraordinary economic growth over the past two decades has given rise to questions as to whether it can sustain this performance indefinitely. Indeed, the process of change in China has occurred at a rate that we Americans have difficulty fathoming. This incredible pace of change has also created formidable problems. Foremost among them are problems such as weak financial structures, inefficient enterprises, growing unemployment and underemployment, especially in rural areas, and worker unrest.

A second set of problems relates to the phenomenon discussed by both Carol Lee Hamrin and Minxin Pei earlier in this volume, that of the emergence over the past two decades of alternative sources of information, civil society, and a middle class. Middle classes do not accept one party rule in which they do not have any opportunity to participate, particularly when they have societal resources to help them organize for collective action. Elsewhere in Asia, in South Korea, Taiwan, Thailand, and Indonesia, for example, this process over a period of three to four decades has led to the replacement of authoritarian governments with democratic ones. Will this happen in China as well? Will the fourth generation be prepared to deal with such a challenge to Communist Party rule? And how will China's internal transformation affect its foreign policy behavior and relations with the United States?

As we stand on the edge of a new century and a new millennium, the future of U.S.–China relations is thus still uncertain. While relations between the two countries may very well improve in the years ahead, perhaps the only thing we can conclude at this point is that, in the words of Zhou Enlai, "It's too soon to tell."

NOTES

1. Interview by Yeeli Hua Zheng [*sic*], Phoenix TV. See "Successful Crawford Meeting Expected: Powell," *People's Daily*, 23 October 2002, <http://english.peopledaily.com.cn/> (23 October 2002).

2. Robert L. Maginnis, "Outside View: China Should Curb N. Korea," *United Press International*, 23 October 2002.

3. Report to Congress of the U.S.–China Security Review Commission: The National Security Implications of the Economic Relationship Between the United States and China, 17 July 2002.

4. "Annual Report on the Military Power of the People's Republic of China," Report to the U.S. Congress, July 2002.

5. "National Defense Authorization Act for FY 2003 Report," U.S. Congress, signed by the President of the United States in December 2002.

Appendix 1

The Three Communiqués

THE JOINT U.S.–CHINA COMMUNIQUÉ
SHANGHAI, FEBRUARY 27, 1972

President Richard Nixon of the United States of America visited the People's Republic of China at the invitation of Premier Chou En-lai of the People's Republic of China from February 21 to February 28, 1972. Accompanying the president were Mrs. Nixon, U.S. Secretary of State William Rogers, Assistant to the President Dr. Henry Kissinger, and other American officials.

President Nixon met with Chairman Mao Tse-tung of the Communist Party of China on February 21. The two leaders had a serious and frank exchange of views on Sino–U.S. relations and world affairs.

During the visit, extensive, earnest and frank discussions were held between President Nixon and Premier Chou En-lai on the normalization of relations between the United States of America and the People's Republic of China, as well as on other matters of interest to both sides. In addition, Secretary of State William Rogers and Foreign Minister Chi Peng-fei held talks in the same spirit.

President Nixon and his party visited Peking and viewed cultural, industrial and agricultural sites, and they also toured Hangchow and Shanghai where, continuing discussions with Chinese leaders, they viewed similar places of interest.

The leaders of the People's Republic of China and the United States found it beneficial to have this opportunity, after so many years without contact, to present candidly to one another their views on a variety of issues. They reviewed the international situation in which important changes and great upheavals are taking place and expounded their respective positions and attitudes.

The U.S. side stated: Peace in Asia and peace in the world requires efforts both to reduce immediate tensions and to eliminate the basic causes of conflict. The United States will work for a just and secure peace: just, because it fulfills the aspirations of peoples and nations for freedom and progress; secure, because it removes the danger of foreign aggression. The United States supports individual freedom and social progress for all the peoples of the world, free of outside pressure or intervention. The United States believes that the effort to reduce tensions is served by improving communication between countries that through accident, miscalculation or misunderstanding. Countries should treat each other with mutual respect and be willing to compete peacefully, letting performance be the ultimate judge. No country should claim infallibility and each country should be prepared to re-examine its own attitudes for the common good. The United States stressed that the peoples of Indochina should be allowed to determine their destiny without outside intervention; its constant primary objective has been a negotiated solution; the eight-point proposal put forward by the Republic of Vietnam and the United States on January 27, 1972 represents a basis for the attainment of that objective; in the absence of a negotiated settlement the United States envisages the ultimate withdrawal of all U.S. forces from the region consistent with the aim of self determination for each country of Indochina. The United States will maintain its close ties with and support for the Republic of Korea; the United States will support efforts of the Republic of Korea to seek a relaxation of tension and increased communication in the Korean peninsula. The United States places the highest value on its friendly relations with Japan; it will continue to develop the existing close bonds. Consistent with the United Nations Security Council Resolution of December 21, 1971, the United States favors the continuation of the ceasefire between India and Pakistan and the withdrawal of all military forces to within their own territories and to their own sides of the ceasefire line in Jammu and Kashmir; the United States supports the right of the peoples of South Asia to shape their own future in peace, free of military threat, and without having the area become the subject of great power rivalry.

The Chinese side stated: Wherever there is oppression, there is resistance. Countries want independence, nations want liberation and the people want revolution—this has become the irresistible trend of history. All nations, big or small, should be equal; big nations should not bully the small and strong nations should not bully the weak. China will never be a superpower and it opposes hegemony and power politics of any kind. The Chinese side stated that it firmly supports the struggles of all the oppressed people and nations for freedom and liberation and that the people of all countries have the right to choose their social systems according to their own wishes and the right to safeguard the independence, sovereignty and territorial integrity of their own countries and oppose foreign aggression, interference, control and subversion. All foreign troops should be withdrawn to their own countries.

The Chinese side expressed its firm support to the peoples of Vietnam, Laos, and Cambodia in their efforts for the attainment of their goal and its firm support to the seven-point proposal of the Provisional Revolutionary Government of the Republic of South Vietnam and the elaboration of February this year on the two key problems in the proposal, and to the Joint Declaration of the Summit Conference of the Indochinese Peoples. It firmly supports the eight-point program for the peaceful unification of Korea put forward by the Government of the Democratic People's Republic of Korea on April 12, 1971, and the stand for the abolition of the "U.N. Commission for the Unification and Rehabilitation of Korea." It firmly opposes the revival and outward expansion of Japanese militarism and firmly supports the Japanese people's desire to build an independent, democratic, peaceful and neutral Japan. It firmly maintains that India and Pakistan should, in accordance with the United Nations resolutions on the India-Pakistan question, immediately withdraw all their forces to their respective territories and to their own sides of the ceasefire line in Jammu and Kashmir and firmly supports the Pakistan Government and people in their struggle to preserve their independence and sovereignty and the people of Jammu and Kashmir in their struggle for the right of self-determination.

There are essential differences between China and the United States in their social systems and foreign policies. However, the two sides agreed that countries, regardless of their social systems, should conduct their relations on the principles of respect for the sovereignty and territorial integrity of all states, nonaggression against other states, noninterference in the internal affairs of other states, equality and mutual benefit, and peaceful coexistence. International disputes should be settled on this basis, without resorting to the use or threat of force. The United States and the People's Republic of China are prepared to apply these principles to their mutual relations.

With these principles of international relations in mind the two sides stated that:

- Progress toward the normalization of relations between China and the United States is in the interests of all countries;
- Both wish to reduce the danger of international military conflict;
- Neither should seek hegemony in the Asia–Pacific region and each is opposed to efforts by any other country or group of countries to establish such hegemony; and
- Neither is prepared to negotiate on behalf of any third party or to enter into agreements or understandings with the other directed at other states.

Both sides are of the view that it would be against the interests of the peoples of the world for any major country to collude with another against other countries, or for major countries to divide up the world into spheres of interest.

The two sides reviewed the longstanding serious disputes between China and the United States. The Chinese reaffirmed its position: The Taiwan question is the crucial question obstructing the normalization of relations between China and the United States; the Government of the People's Republic of China is the sole legal government of China; Taiwan is a province of China which has long been returned to the motherland; the liberation of Taiwan is China's internal affair in which no other country has the right to interfere; and all U.S. forces and military installations must be withdrawn from Taiwan. The Chinese Government firmly opposes any activities which aim at the creation of "one China, one Taiwan," "one China, two governments," "two Chinas," and "independent Taiwan," or advocate that "the status of Taiwan remains to be determined."

The U.S. side declared: The United States acknowledges that all Chinese on either side of the Taiwan Strait maintain there is but one China and that Taiwan is a part of China. The United States Government does not challenge that position. It reaffirms its interest in a peaceful settlement of the Taiwan question by the Chinese themselves. With this prospect in mind, it affirms the ultimate objective of the withdrawal of all U.S. forces and military installations from Taiwan. In the meantime, it will progressively reduce its forces and military installations on Taiwan as the tension in the area diminishes.

The two sides agreed that it is desirable to broaden the understanding between the two peoples. To this end, they discussed specific areas in such fields as science, technology, culture, sports and journalism, in which people-to-people contacts and exchanges would be mutually beneficial. Each side undertakes to facilitate the further development of such contacts and exchanges.

Both sides view bilateral trade as another area from which mutual benefit can be derived, and agreed that economic relations based on equality and mutual benefit are in the interest of the peoples of the two countries. They agree to facilitate the progressive development of trade between their two countries.

The two sides agreed that they will stay in contact through various channels, including the sending of a senior U.S. representative to Peking from time to time for concrete consultations to further the normalization of relations between the two countries and continue to exchange views on issues of common interest.

The two sides expressed the hope that the gains achieved during this visit would open up new prospects for the relations between the two countries. They believe that the normalization of relations between the two countries is not only in the interest of the Chinese and American peoples but also contributes to the relaxation of tension in Asia and the world.

President Nixon, Mrs. Nixon, and the American party expressed their appreciation for the gracious hospitality shown them by the Government and people of the People's Republic of China.

JOINT COMMUNIQUÉ ON THE ESTABLISHMENT OF DIPLOMATIC RELATIONS BETWEEN THE UNITED STATES OF AMERICA AND THE PEOPLE'S REPUBLIC OF CHINA JANUARY 1, 1979

(THE COMMUNIQUÉ WAS RELEASED ON DECEMBER 15, 1978, IN WASHINGTON AND PEKING)

The United States of America and the People's Republic of China have agreed to recognize each other and to establish diplomatic relations as of January 1, 1979.

The United States of America recognizes the Government of the People's Republic of China as the sole legal Government of China. Within this context, the people of the United States will maintain cultural, commercial, and other unofficial relations with the people of Taiwan.

The United States of America and the People's Republic of China reaffirm the principles agreed on by the two sides in the Shanghai Communiqué and emphasize once again that:

- Both wish to reduce the danger of international military conflict.
- Neither should seek hegemony in the Asia-Pacific region or in any other region of the world and each is opposed to efforts by any other country or group of countries to establish such hegemony.
- Neither is prepared to negotiate on behalf of any third party or to enter into agreements or understandings with the other directed at other states.
- The Government of the United States of America acknowledges the Chinese position that there is but one China and Taiwan is part of China.
- Both believe that normalization of Sino–American relations is not only in the interest of the Chinese and American peoples but also contributes to the cause of peace in Asia and the world.

The United States of America and the People's Republic of China will exchange Ambassadors and establish Embassies on March 1, 1979.

U.S.–PRC JOINT COMMUNIQUÉ
AUGUST 17, 1982

1. In the Joint Communiqué on the Establishment of Diplomatic Relations on January 1, 1979, issued by the Government of the United States of America and the Government of the People's Republic of China, the United States of America recognized the Government of the People's Republic of China as the sole legal government of China, and it acknowledged the Chinese position that there is but one China and Taiwan is part of China. Within that context, the two sides agreed that the people of the United States would continue to maintain cultural, commercial, and other unofficial relations with the people of Taiwan. On this basis, relations between the United States and China were normalized.

2. The question of United States arms sales to Taiwan was not settled in the course of negotiations between the two countries on establishing diplomatic relations. The two sides held differing positions, and the Chinese side stated that it would raise the issue again following normalization. Recognizing that this issue would seriously hamper the development of United States–China relations, they have held further discussions on it, during and since the meetings between President Ronald Reagan and Premier Zhao Ziyang and between Secretary of State Alexander M. Haig Jr., and Vice Premier and Foreign Minister Huang Hua in October 1981.

3. Respect for each other's sovereignty and territorial integrity and noninterference each other's internal affairs constitute the fundamental principles guiding United States–China relations. These principles were confirmed in the Shanghai Communiqué of February 28, 1972 and reaffirmed in the Joint Communiqué on the Establishment of Diplomatic Relations which came into effect on January 1, 1973. Both sides emphatically state that these principles continue to govern all aspects of their relations.

4. The Chinese government reiterates that the question of Taiwan is China's internal affair. The Message to the Compatriots in Taiwan issued by China on January 1, 1979, promulgated a fundamental policy of striving for peaceful reunification of the Motherland. The Nine-Point Proposal put forward by China on September 30, 1981 represented a further major effort under this fundamental policy to strive for a peaceful solution to the Taiwan question.

5. The United States Government attaches great importance to its relations with China, and reiterates that it has no intention of infringing on Chinese sovereignty and territorial integrity, or interfering in China's inter-

nal affairs, or pursuing a policy of "two Chinas" or "one China, one Taiwan." The United States Government understands and appreciates the Chinese policy of striving for a peaceful resolution of the Taiwan question as indicated in China's Message to Compatriots in Taiwan issued on January 1, 1979 and the Nine-Point Proposal put forward by China on September 30, 1981. The new situation which has emerged with regard to the Taiwan question also provides favorable conditions for the settlement of United States–China differences over the question of United States arms sales to Taiwan.

6. Having in mind the foregoing statements of both sides, the United States Government states that it does not seek to carry out a long-term policy of arms sales to Taiwan, that its arms sales to Taiwan will not exceed, either in qualitative or in quantitative terms, the level of those supplied in recent years since the establishment of diplomatic relations between the United States and China, and that it intends to reduce gradually its sales of arms to Taiwan, leading over a period of time to a final resolution. In so stating, the United States acknowledges China's consistent position regarding the thorough settlement of this issue.

7. In order to bring about, over a period of time, a final settlement of the question of United States arms sales to Taiwan, which is an issue rooted in history, the two governments will make every effort to adopt measures and create conditions conducive to the thorough settlement of this issue.

8. The development of United States–China relations is not only in the interest of the two peoples but also conducive to peace and stability in the world. The two sides are determined, on the principle of equality and mutual benefit, to strengthen their ties to the economic, cultural, educational, scientific, technological, and other fields and make strong, joint efforts for the continued development of relations between the governments and peoples of the United States and China.

9. In order to bring about the healthy development of United States–China relations, maintain world peace and oppose aggression and expansion, the two governments reaffirm the principles agreed on by the two sides in the Shanghai Communiqué and the Joint Communiqué on the Establishment of Diplomatic Relations. The two sides will maintain contact and hold appropriate consultations on bilateral and international issues of common interest.

Appendix 2

U.S.–China Security Review Commission Report

REPORT TO CONGRESS OF THE U.S.–CHINA SECURITY REVIEW COMMISSION (JULY 2002)

The National Security Implications of the Economic Relationship between the United States and China—Executive Summary

Relations between the United States and China during the last half-century have not always been smooth. The two countries have sharply contrasting worldviews, competing geostrategic interests, and opposing political systems. More recently, bilateral ties have centered on rapidly growing economic interactions that have muted political differences. For the moment, these relations have not softened China's egregious behavior on human rights nor changed its strategic perceptions that the United States is its principal obstacle to growing regional influence. No one can reliably predict whether relations between the United States and China will remain contentious or grow into a cooperative relationship molded by either converging ideologies or respect for ideological differences, compatible regional interests, and a mutually beneficial economic relationship.

However the relationship develops, it will have a profound impact on the course of the twenty-first century. The policies pursued today by both China and the United States will affect future relations. The Congress created the U.S.–China Security Review Commission to assess "the national security implications and impact of the bilateral trade and economic relationship between the United States and the People's Republic of China" and to report its conclusions annually to the Congress. It specifically directed the Commission to focus on our deepening economic, trade, and financial linkages with China. The Congress wanted the Commission to evaluate whether our economic policies with China harm or help United States national security and, based on that assessment, to make recommendations in those areas that will improve our nation's interests.

National security has come to include military, economic and political relationships. At any time, one of these concerns may dominate. They interact with one another and affect our overall security and well-being. Neglect of any one element will diminish our overall security as a nation. The United States must be attentive to the strength and readiness of our military forces, the health of our economy, and the vibrancy of our political relationships.

The Congress also asked the Commission to include in its Report "a full analysis, along with conclusions and recommendations for legislative and administrative actions." This is the Commission's first Report. In keeping with the Congressional mandate, this Report provides a comprehensive analysis of the Commission's year-long review of U.S.–China relations, the principal findings that emerged from that investigation, and the recommendations or measures the Commission believes should be implemented to help safeguard our national security in the years ahead. This initial Report provides a baseline against which to measure and assess year-to-year changes in the relationship.

MAIN THEMES

Our relationship with China is one of the most important bilateral relationships for our nation. If it is not handled properly, it can cause significant economic and security problems for our country. China is emerging as a global economic and military power, and the United States has played, and continues to play a major role in China's development.

China's foreign trade has skyrocketed over the past twenty years (from approximately $20 billion in the late 1970s to $475 billion in 2000). Our trade deficit with China has grown at a sharp rate, from $11.5 billion in 1990 to $85 billion in 2000. Foreign investment—with America a leading investor—grew apace. This trade and investment has helped to strengthen China both economically and militarily.

America's policy of economic engagement with China rests on a belief that the transition to a free market economy and the development of the rule of law in China's business sector would likely lead to more political and social openness and even democracy. This belief, along with the desire to expand American commercial interests, drove U.S. support for China's entry into the World Trade Organization (WTO). Many also believe that a more prosperous China will be a more peaceful country, especially if it is fully integrated into the Pacific and world economies.

But these are hypotheses, and many leading experts are convinced that certain aspects of our policy of engagement have been a mistake. They argue that the PRC faces enormous economic and social problems, that its leaders are intractably antidemocratic, that they are hostile to the United States and its prominent role in Asia, and that we are strengthening a country that could challenge us economically, politically and militarily.

The Commission does not believe that anyone can confidently forecast the future of China and the U.S.–China relationship, and contends that while we may work and hope for the best, our policymakers should prepare for all contingencies.

Over the past twenty years, China has created a more market-based economy and allowed more social and economic freedom. Chinese participation in international security and economic regimes has grown. On the other hand, China has made little progress toward granting its citizens political and religious freedom, and protecting human and labor rights. In fact, the government has notably increased its repression of some religious practices, including its brutal campaign against the Falun Gong.

Chinese leaders have repeatedly stressed to their Communist Party supporters and the Chinese people that they have no desire to repeat in China the political and economic collapse that took place in the former Soviet Union. They seek to maintain and strengthen the Communist Party's political and social control while permitting freer economic activity. They consistently limit the freedom of the Chinese people to obtain and exchange information, practice their religious faith, to publicly express their convictions, and to join freely organized labor unions. Chinese leaders frequently use nationalistic themes to rally support for their actions, including crackdowns on dissenters.

China is thus embarked on a highly questionable effort—to open its economy but not its political system—the outcome of which will influence the destinies of many countries, including our own. If the economy fails, or if the Chinese people demand full freedom instead of merely a taste of it, then the leaders will have to choose between reasserting central control and granting greater political and social freedom, with a consequent weakening of their own authority. On the other hand, if China becomes rich but not free, the United States may face a wealthy, powerful nation that could be hostile toward our democratic values, to us, and in direct competition with us for influence in Asia and beyond.

American policy makers must take these scenarios seriously, and to that end the Commission has established benchmarks against which to measure future change. There are important areas in which Chinese policy runs directly counter to U.S. national security interests, such as not controlling exports that contribute to the proliferation of weapons of mass destruction, its close relations with terrorist-sponsoring states like Iran, Iraq, Syria, Libya, Sudan, and

North Korea, its expanding long-range missile forces, its threatening policies toward Taiwan, and its pursuit of both asymmetric warfare capabilities and modern military technology that could menace American military forces.

China's leaders view the United States as a partner of convenience, useful for its capital, technology, know-how and market. They often describe the United States as China's long-term competitor for regional and global military and economic influence. Much rhetoric and a considerable volume of official writings support this hypothesis. The recent empirical study of Chinese newspapers' coverage of the United States, conducted by University of Maryland scholars for the Commission, found a divided perspective: articles in these newspapers, which we believe generally represent the views of the leadership, are consistently positive on trade and investment matters and applaud Sino–U.S. cooperation in these areas. In contrast, their coverage of U.S. foreign policy is largely negative and frequently depicts the United States as hegemonic and unilateralist.

In time we will learn whether China is to become a responsible world power or an aggressive, wealthy dictatorship, and whether the Communist Party maintains its monopoly of political power or shares it with the Chinese people. We will also learn whether the Chinese economy flourishes or stumbles and collapses under the burden of state-owned industries, a weak banking system, enormous debt, wide-scale corruption, social dislocation, and the new challenges of international competition brought about by its WTO entry.

Current U.S. policies and laws fail to adequately monitor the transfers of economic resources and security-related technologies to China, considering the substantial uncertainties and challenges to U.S. national interests in this relationship. This Report attempts to begin to address these uncertainties, trends, and challenges in a systematic manner. It proceeds on the premise that far more prudence must be displayed and far better understanding developed on the part of the Congress on the full extent of this relationship and its impact on U.S. interests. In addition, too little attention has been devoted to the adverse impact of recent Chinese economic strength on our Asian allies and friends. The Commission believes the United States must develop a better understanding of the vulnerabilities and needs of our Asian allies and friends, and must carefully construct policies to protect and nurture those relationships.

SUMMARY OF RECOMMENDATIONS

The Commission has identified its key findings and recommendations with each chapter in this Report. The Commission developed more than forty recommendations that are listed with each of the ten chapters. We have prepared a separate classified report providing additional details and recommendations. Here, we highlight and summarize those recommendations we believe are the highest priority and which we recommend for immediate action. A more extended analysis is contained in each of the Report's ten chapters.

Conflicting National Perspectives

The United States Government is poorly organized to manage our increasingly complex relationship with China. We are not adequately informed about developments within China and about their leaders' perceptions of the United States and we dedicate insufficient resources to understand China. Because Chinese strategic thinking and analysis of military planning differ markedly from our own, our incomplete understanding enhances the possibilities for miscalculation, misunderstanding, and potential conflict.

- Recommendation 1: The U.S. Government should expand its collection, translation and analysis of open source Chinese-language materials, and make them available to the larger community. Despite two studies advocating an improved collection of Chinese materials at the Library of Congress, its collection is nearly unusable and shameful. Congress should provide funds to implement recommendations already submitted by the two previous studies. In addition, the Commission recommends increased funding for Chinese language training and area studies programs, similar to the program in the National Defense Education Act of 1958, and incentives for post-secondary graduates to participate in government service. The relevant executive branch agencies should report annually to the Congress on steps taken to rectify this situation.
- Recommendation 2: The United States should develop a comprehensive inventory of official government-to-government and U.S. Government-funded programs with China. The President should designate an executive branch agency to coordinate the compilation of a database of all such cooperative programs. The database should include a full description of each program, its achievements to date, and the benefits to the United States and should be prepared annually in both classified and unclassified forms. The Commission further recommends that the executive branch prepare a biannual report, beginning in 2004, on the cooperative Science and Technology (S&T) programs with China patterned on the report submitted to Congress in May 2002 at the request of Senator Robert C. Byrd. The President should establish a working group to set standards for S&T transfers, monitor the programs, and coordinate with the intelligence agencies.

- Recommendation 3: The Commission recommends that Congress encourage the Department of Defense to renew efforts to develop military-to-military confidence building measures (CBMs) within the context of a strategic dialogue with China and based strictly on the principles of reciprocity, transparency, consistency, and mutual benefit.

Managing U.S.–China Economic Relations (Trade and Investment)

The United States has played a major role in China's rise as an economic power. We are China's largest export market and a key investor in its economy. Fueled by China's virtually inexhaustible supply of low-cost labor and large inflows of foreign direct investment (FDI), the U.S. trade deficit with China has grown at a furious pace—from $11.5 billion in 1990 to $85 billion in 2000. The U.S. trade deficit with China is not only our largest deficit in absolute terms but also the most unbalanced trading relationship the United States maintains. U.S. trade with China is only 5 percent of total U.S. trade with the world but our trade deficit with China is 19 percent of the total U.S. trade deficit. U.S. exports to China are only 2 percent of total U.S. exports to the world, while we import over 40 percent of China's exports.

Foreign direct investment has helped China leapfrog forward both economically and technologically. These developments have provided China with large dollar reserves, advanced technologies, and greater R&D capacity, each of which has helped make China an important world manufacturing center and a growing center of R&D, which are contributing to its military-industrial modernization.

U.S. companies have difficulty competing with Chinese based companies, in large part, because the cost of labor in China is depressed through low wages and denial of worker rights. Essentially, Chinese workers do not have the ability to negotiate their wages. Attracted in part by the low wages in China, a growing number of U.S. manufacturers are now operating in China, many of whom are utilizing China as an "export platform" to compete in U.S. and global markets.

China's large trade surplus with the United States, the inflow of U.S. private investment into China, and China's access to U.S. capital markets each contributes, directly or indirectly, to China's economic growth and military modernization.

- Recommendation 4: The Commission recommends the creation of a federally mandated corporate reporting system that would gather appropriate data to provide a more comprehensive understanding of the U.S. trade and investment relationship with China. The reporting system should include reports from U.S. companies doing business in China on their initial investment, any transfers of technology, offset or R&D cooperation associated with any investment, and the impact on job relocation and production capacity from the United States or U.S. firms overseas resulting from any investment in China.

- Recommendation 5: The Commission recommends that the United States make full and active use of various trade tools including special safeguards provisions in the WTO to gain full compliance by China with its World Trade Organization (WTO) accession agreement.

China's WTO Membership: Conflicting Goals

The United States and China hold differing goals for China's membership in the WTO. (The Chinese saying for this situation is: "same bed, different dreams.") China's leadership sought WTO membership to further the nation's economic reform and growth through export production and the accumulation of foreign investment, capital, and technology in order to become a world power. U.S. support for China's WTO membership was intended to enhance market access for U.S. goods and services, and also to promote internal economic, political and civil reforms, including a more open society.

China has instituted legal reforms to supervise foreign direct investment (FDI), financial markets and private businesses in order to stimulate trade and investment and fulfill the country's WTO commitments. The development of a commercial rule of law in China faces numerous obstacles, including the lack of an independent judiciary and trained judges, local protectionism, and widespread corruption. Despite some advances in commercial legal reforms, China remains grossly deficient in granting its citizens civil and political freedoms, and makes widespread use of prison labor.

- Recommendation 6: The Commission recommends that Congress renew the Super 301 provision of U.S. trade law and request the Administration to identify and report on other tools that would be most effective in opening China's market to U.S. exports if China fails to comply with its WTO commitments. In examining these tools, priority should be given to those industry sectors where China expects rapid economic growth in exports to the U.S. market.
- Recommendation 7: Congress should authorize and appropriate additional funds to strengthen the Commerce Department's support for commercial rule of law reform in China, including intellectual property rights and WTO implementation assistance, and to strengthen the Department of State's promotion of capacity-building programs in the rule of law, administrative reform, judicial reform and related areas.

- Recommendation 8: The United States should improve enforcement against imports of Chinese goods made from prison labor by shifting the burden of proof to U.S. importers and by more stringent requirements relating to visits to Chinese facilities suspected of producing and exporting prison-made goods to the United States. (Note: The Commission made recommendations to Congress on this issue in a May 2002 letter).
- Recommendation 9: The Commission recommends that Congress request the annual Trade Promotion Coordination Committee (TPCC) report prepared by the Department of Commerce include an assessment of China's progress in compliance with its WTO commitments, recommendations on initiatives to facilitate compliance, and a survey of market access attained by key U.S. industry sectors in China, including agriculture. The report should include comparisons of U.S. market access in those key industry sectors with those gained by the European Union and Japan.
- Recommendation 10: The Commission recommends that Congress urge the U.S. Trade Representative (USTR) to request WTO consultations on China's noncompliance with its obligations under the Trade-related Aspects of Intellectual Property Rights (TRIPS) Agreement, particularly its inadequate enforcement, to deter China's counterfeiting and piracy of motion pictures and other video products. If China fails to respond, Congress should encourage the USTR to request a WTO dispute settlement panel be convened on the matter.
- Recommendation 11: Congress mandated the Commission to evaluate and make recommendations on invoking Article XXI of the General Agreement on Tariffs and Trade (GATT), relating to security exceptions from GATT obligations. The Commission believes that the steel industry is a possible candidate for using Article XXI. If the Administration's current safeguard measures prove ineffective, the Commission recommends that Congress consider using Article XXI to ensure the survival of the U.S. steel industry.

Accessing U.S. Capital Markets

Chinese firms raising capital or trading their securities in U.S. markets have almost exclusively been large state-owned enterprises, some of which have ties to China's military and intelligence services. There is a growing concern that some of these firms may be assisting in the proliferation of weapons of mass destruction or ballistic missile delivery systems. The United States lacks adequate institutional mechanisms to monitor national security concerns raised by certain Chinese and other foreign entities accessing the U.S. debt and equity markets. We also lack sufficient disclosure requirements to inform the investing public of the potential risks associated with investing in such entities.

- Recommendation 12: The Commission recommends that foreign entities seeking to raise capital or trade their securities in U.S. markets be required to disclose information to investors regarding their business activities in countries subject to U.S. economic sanctions.
- Recommendation 13: The Commission recommends that the Treasury Department, in coordination with other relevant agencies, assess whether China or any other country associated with the proliferation of weapons of mass destruction or ballistic missile delivery systems are accessing U.S. capital markets and make this information available to the Securities Exchange Commission (SEC), state public pension plans, and U.S. investors. Entities sanctioned by the Department of State for such activities should be denied access to U.S. markets.

Proliferation of Weapons of Mass Destruction

China fails to control the export of dual-use items that contribute to the proliferation of weapons of mass destruction and their delivery systems. China is a leading international source of missile-related technologies. Its proliferation activities with terrorist-sponsoring and other states, despite commitments to the United States to cease such activities, present serious problems for U.S. national security interests, particularly in the Middle East and Asia.

- Recommendation 14: The Commission recommends that the President be provided an extensive range of options to penalize foreign countries for violating commitments or agreements on proliferation involving weapons of mass destruction and technologies and delivery systems relating to them. All current statutes dealing with proliferation should be amended to include a separate authorization for the President to implement economic and other sanctions against offending countries, including quantitative and qualitative export and import restrictions, restricting access to U.S. capital markets, controlling technology transfers, and limiting U.S. direct investment.
- Recommendation 15: The United States should work with the United Nations Security Council and other appropriate inter-governmental organizations to formulate a framework for effective multilateral action to counter proliferation of weapons of mass destruction and their delivery systems. Member states found in violation of the agreed framework should be subject to international sanctions.

- Recommendation 16: The United States should continue to prohibit satellite launch cooperation with China until it puts into place an effective export-control system consistent with its November 2000 commitment to the United States to restrict proliferation of weapons of mass destruction and associated technologies to other countries and entities.

Cross-Strait and Regional Relations

Cross-strait relations are a major potential flashpoint in U.S.–China relations. Economic and people-to-people interactions between Taiwan and the Mainland have increased dramatically in recent years, raising prospects that such interactions could help ameliorate cross-strait political tensions. At the same time, China is enhancing its capability to carry out an attack across the Taiwan Strait with special operations, air, navy and missile forces. It continues to deploy short- and intermediate-range missiles opposite Taiwan and although the threat of an immediate attack appears to be low, this buildup appears designed to forestall pro-independence political movements in Taiwan and help bring about an eventual end to the Island's continued separate status.

China's economic integration with its neighbors in East Asia raises the prospects of an Asian economic area dominated or significantly influenced by China. The United States has an interest in China's integration in Asia if it gives all parties a stake in avoiding hostilities. Nonetheless, U.S. influence in the area could wane to a degree, particularly on economic and trade matters.

- Recommendation 17: The Commission recommends that the Department of Defense continue its substantive military dialogue with Taiwan and conduct exchanges on issues ranging from threat analysis, doctrine, and force planning.
- Recommendation 18: The Commission recommends making permanent those provisions in the fiscal years 2001 and 2002 Foreign Operations Appropriations Acts providing for executive branch briefings to the Congress on regular discussions between the administration and the government on Taiwan pertaining to U.S. arms sales to Taiwan.
- Recommendation 19: The Commission believes that the Congress should encourage the Administration to initiate consultations with other Asian countries to assess and make recommendations on the impact of the "hollowing out" phenomenon with respect to China on regional economies and on U.S. economic relations with the region.

China's Military Economy

China's official defense spending has expanded by more than one-third in the past two years. The Commission estimates that China's official defense budget represents about one-third of its actual spending level. Its ability to increase defense spending in the face of competing priorities is supported by its rapid economic growth. China has the largest standing army in the world and ranks second in actual aggregate spending. The military's role in China's economy has been reduced in recent years, but the military derives extensive financial and technological benefits from the growth and modernization of the domestic economy, which is designed to serve it.

- Recommendation 20: The Commission recommends that the Secretary of Defense prepare a biannual report on critical elements of the U.S. defense industrial base that are becoming dependent on Chinese imports or Chinese-owned companies. The Department of Defense should also update its acquisition guidelines and develop information from defense contractors on any dependency for critical parts of essential U.S. weapons systems.

Technology Transfers and Military Acquisitions

China has a well-established policy and program to acquire advanced technologies for its industrial development, military capabilities and intelligence services. Over the next ten years, China intends to acquire an industrial capability to build advanced conventional and strategic weapons systems. Current U.S. policies do not adequately consider the impact of the transfers of commercial and security-related technologies to China.

- Recommendation 21: The Commission recommends that the Department of Defense and the FBI jointly assess China's targeting of sensitive U.S. weapons-related technologies, the means employed to gain access to these technologies and the steps that have been and should be taken to deny access and acquisition. This assessment should include an annual report on Chinese companies and Chinese PLA-affiliated companies operating in the United States. Such reports are mandated by statute but have never been provided to Congress.

The Commission cannot forecast with certainty the future course of U.S.–China relations. Nor can we predict with any confidence how China and Chinese society will develop in the next ten to twenty years. We do know that

China now ranks among our most important and most troubling bilateral relationships and believe that China's importance to the United States will increase in the years ahead. As its economy and military grow and its influence expands, China's actions will carry increased importance for the American people and for our national interests.

For this reason, the Commission believes that there is a pressing need to fully understand the increasingly complex economic, political and military challenges posed by China's drive toward modernity. To gain such comprehension will require the allocation of more resources and the elevation of China in our foreign and national security priorities. The Commission hopes that U.S.–China relations will develop in a positive direction but we must urge caution that this outcome, though preferred, may not happen. The United States must, therefore, be prepared for all possible contingencies.

Appendix 3

U.S. National Security Strategy, 2002

THE NATIONAL SECURITY STRATEGY
OF THE UNITED STATES OF AMERICA
SEPTEMBER 2002

The great struggles of the twentieth century between liberty and totalitarianism ended with a decisive victory for the forces of freedom—and a single sustainable model for national success: freedom, democracy, and free enterprise. In the twenty-first century, only nations that share a commitment to protecting basic human rights and guaranteeing political and economic freedom will be able to unleash the potential of their people and assure their future prosperity. People everywhere want to be able to speak freely; choose who will govern them; worship as they please; educate their children—male and female; own property; and enjoy the benefits of their labor. These values of freedom are right and true for every person, in every society—and the duty of protecting these values against their enemies is the common calling of freedom-loving people across the globe and across the ages.

Today, the United States enjoys a position of unparalleled military strength and great economic and political influence. In keeping with our heritage and principles, we do not use our strength to press for unilateral advantage. We seek instead to create a balance of power that favors human freedom: conditions in which all nations and all societies can choose for themselves the rewards and challenges of political and economic liberty. In a world that is safe, people will be able to make their own lives better. We will defend the peace by fighting terrorists and tyrants. We will preserve the peace by building good relations among the great powers. We will extend the peace by encouraging free and open societies on every continent.

Defending our Nation against its enemies is the first and fundamental commitment of the Federal Government. Today, that task has changed dramatically. Enemies in the past needed great armies and great industrial capabilities to endanger America. Now, shadowy networks of individuals can bring great chaos and suffering to our shores for less than it costs to purchase a single tank. Terrorists are organized to penetrate open societies and to turn the power of modern technologies against us.

To defeat this threat we must make use of every tool in our arsenal—military power, better homeland defenses, law enforcement, intelligence, and vigorous efforts to cut off terrorist financing. The war against terrorists of global reach is a global enterprise of uncertain duration. America will help nations that need our assistance in combating terror. And America will hold to account nations that are compromised by terror, including those who harbor terrorists—because the allies of terror are the enemies of civilization. The United States and countries cooperating with us must not allow the terrorists to develop new home bases. Together, we will seek to deny them sanctuary at every turn.

The gravest danger our Nation faces lies at the crossroads of radicalism and technology. Our enemies have openly declared that they are seeking weapons of mass destruction, and evidence indicates that they are doing so with determination. The United States will not allow these efforts to succeed. We will build defenses against ballistic missiles and other means of delivery. We will cooperate with other nations to deny, contain, and curtail our enemies' efforts to acquire dangerous technologies. And, as a matter of common sense and self-defense, America will act against such emerging threats before they are fully formed. We cannot defend America and our friends by hoping for the best. So we must be prepared to defeat our enemies' plans, using the best intelligence and proceeding with deliberation. History will judge harshly those who saw this coming danger but failed to act. In the new world we have entered, the only path to peace and security is the path of action.

As we defend the peace, we will also take advantage of an historic opportunity to preserve the peace. Today, the international community has the best chance since the rise of the nation–state in the seventeenth century to build a world where great powers compete in peace instead of continually prepare for war. Today, the world's great powers find ourselves on the same side—united by common dangers of terrorist violence and chaos. The United States will build on these common interests to promote global security. We are also increasingly united by common values. Russia is in the midst of a hopeful transition, reaching for its democratic future and a partner in the war on terror. Chinese leaders are discovering that economic freedom is the only source of national wealth. In time, they will find that social and political freedom is the only source of national greatness. America will encourage the advancement of democracy and economic openness in both nations, because these are the best foundations for domestic stability and international order. We will strongly resist aggression from other great powers—even as we welcome their peaceful pursuit of prosperity, trade, and cultural advancement.

Finally, the United States will use this moment of opportunity to extend the benefits of freedom across the globe. We will actively work to bring the hope of democracy, development, free markets, and free trade to every corner of the world. The events of September 11, 2001, taught us that weak states, like Afghanistan, can pose as great a danger to our national interests as strong states. Poverty does not make poor people into terrorists and murderers. Yet poverty, weak institutions, and corruption can make weak states vulnerable to terrorist networks and drug cartels within their borders.

The United States will stand beside any nation determined to build a better future by seeking the rewards of liberty for its people. Free trade and free markets have proven their ability to lift whole societies out of poverty—so the United States will work with individual nations, entire regions, and the entire global trading community to build a world that trades in freedom and therefore grows in prosperity. The United States will deliver greater development assistance through the New Millennium Challenge Account to nations that govern justly, invest in their people, and encourage economic freedom. We will also continue to lead the world in efforts to reduce the terrible toll of HIV/AIDS and other infectious diseases.

In building a balance of power that favors freedom, the United States is guided by the conviction that all nations have important responsibilities. Nations that enjoy freedom must actively fight terror. Nations that depend on international stability must help prevent the spread of weapons of mass destruction. Nations that seek international aid must govern themselves wisely, so that aid is well spent. For freedom to thrive, accountability must be expected and required.

We are also guided by the conviction that no nation can build a safer, better world alone. Alliances and multilateral institutions can multiply the strength of freedom-loving nations. The United States is committed to lasting institutions like the United Nations, the World Trade Organization, the Organization of American States, and NATO as well as other long-standing alliances. Coalitions of the willing can augment these permanent institutions. In all cases, international obligations are to be taken seriously. They are not to be undertaken symbolically to rally support for an ideal without furthering its attainment.

Freedom is the non-negotiable demand of human dignity; the birthright of every person—in every civilization. Throughout history, freedom has been threatened by war and terror; it has been challenged by the clashing wills of powerful states and the evil designs of tyrants; and it has been tested by wide-spread poverty and disease. Today, humanity holds in its hands the opportunity to further freedom's triumph over all these foes. The United States welcomes our responsibility to lead in this great mission.

President George W. Bush
The White House,
September 17, 2002

I. OVERVIEW OF AMERICA'S INTERNATIONAL STRATEGY

"Our Nation's cause has always been larger than our Nation's defense. We fight, as we always fight, for a just peace—a peace that favors liberty. We will defend the peace against the threats from terrorists and tyrants. We will preserve the peace by building good relations among the great powers. And we will extend the peace by encouraging free and open societies on every continent."

President George W. Bush
West Point, New York
June 1, 2002

The United States possesses unprecedented—and unequaled—strength and influence in the world. Sustained by faith in the principles of liberty, and the value of a free society, this position comes with unparalleled responsibilities, obligations, and opportunity. The great strength of this nation must be used to promote a balance of power that favors freedom.

For most of the twentieth century, the world was divided by a great struggle over ideas: destructive totalitarian visions versus freedom and equality.

That great struggle is over. The militant visions of class, nation, and race which promised utopia and delivered misery have been defeated and discredited. America is now threatened less by conquering states than we are by failing ones. We are menaced less by fleets and armies than by catastrophic technologies in the hands of the embittered few. We must defeat these threats to our Nation, allies, and friends.

This is also a time of opportunity for America. We will work to translate this moment of influence into decades of peace, prosperity, and liberty. The U.S. national security strategy will be based on a distinctly American internationalism that reflects the union of our values and our national interests. The aim of this strategy is to help make the world not just safer but better. Our goals on the path to progress are clear: political and economic freedom, peaceful relations with other states, and respect for human dignity.

And this path is not America's alone. It is open to all. To achieve these goals, the United States will:

- champion aspirations for human dignity;
- strengthen alliances to defeat global terrorism and work to prevent attacks against us and our friends;
- work with others to defuse regional conflicts;
- prevent our enemies from threatening us, our allies, and our friends, with weapons of mass destruction;
- ignite a new era of global economic growth through free markets and free trade;
- expand the circle of development by opening societies and building the infrastructure of democracy;
- develop agendas for cooperative action with other main centers of global power; and
- transform America's national security institutions to meet the challenges and opportunities of the twenty-first century.

II. CHAMPION ASPIRATIONS FOR HUMAN DIGNITY

"Some worry that it is somehow undiplomatic or impolite to speak the language of right and wrong. I disagree. Different circumstances require different methods, but not different moralities."

President George W. Bush
West Point, New York
June 1, 2002

In pursuit of our goals, our first imperative is to clarify what we stand for: the United States must defend liberty and justice because these principles are right and true for all people everywhere. No nation owns these aspirations, and no nation is exempt from them. Fathers and mothers in all societies want their children to be educated and to live free from poverty and violence. No people on earth yearn to be oppressed, aspire to servitude, or eagerly await the midnight knock of the secret police.

America must stand firmly for the nonnegotiable demands of human dignity: the rule of law; limits on the absolute power of the state; free speech; freedom of worship; equal justice; respect for women; religious and ethnic tolerance; and respect for private property.

These demands can be met in many ways. America's constitution has served us well. Many other nations, with different histories and cultures, facing different circumstances, have successfully incorporated these core principles into their own systems of governance. History has not been kind to those nations which ignored or flouted the rights and aspirations of their people.

America's experience as a great multi-ethnic democracy affirms our conviction that people of many heritages and faiths can live and prosper in peace. Our own history is a long struggle to live up to our ideals. But even in our worst moments, the principles enshrined in the Declaration of Independence were there to guide us. As a result, America is not just a stronger, but is a freer and more just society.

Today, these ideals are a lifeline to lonely defenders of liberty. And when openings arrive, we can encourage change—as we did in central and eastern Europe between 1989 and 1991, or in Belgrade in 2000.When we see democratic processes take hold among our friends in Taiwan or in the Republic of Korea, and see elected leaders replace generals in Latin America and Africa, we see examples of how authoritarian systems can evolve, marrying local history and traditions with the principles we all cherish.

Embodying lessons from our past and using the opportunity we have today, the national security strategy of the United States must start from these core beliefs and look outward for possibilities to expand liberty.

Our principles will guide our government's decisions about international cooperation, the character of our foreign assistance, and the allocation of resources. They will guide our actions and our words in international bodies.

We will:

- speak out honestly about violations of the nonnegotiable demands of human dignity using our voice and vote in international institutions to advance freedom;
- use our foreign aid to promote freedom and support those who struggle non-violently for it, ensuring that nations moving toward democracy are rewarded for the steps they take;
- make freedom and the development of democratic institutions key themes in our bilateral relations, seeking solidarity and cooperation from other democracies while we press governments that deny human rights to move toward a better future; and
- take special efforts to promote freedom of religion and conscience and defend it from encroachment by repressive governments.

We will champion the cause of human dignity and oppose those who resist it.

III. STRENGTHEN ALLIANCES TO DEFEAT GLOBAL TERRORISM AND WORK TO PREVENT ATTACKS AGAINST US AND OUR FRIENDS

"Just three days removed from these events, Americans do not yet have the distance of history. But our responsibility to history is already clear: to answer these attacks and rid the world of evil. War has been waged against us by stealth and deceit and murder. This nation is peaceful, but fierce when stirred to anger. The conflict was begun on the timing and terms of others. It will end in a way, and at an hour, of our choosing."

President George W. Bush
Washington, D.C. (The National Cathedral)
September 14, 2001

The United States of America is fighting a war against terrorists of global reach. The enemy is not a single political regime or person or religion or ideology. The enemy is terrorism—premeditated, politically motivated violence perpetrated against innocents.

In many regions, legitimate grievances prevent the emergence of a lasting peace. Such grievances deserve to be, and must be, addressed within a political process. But no cause justifies terror. The United States will make no concessions to terrorist demands and strike no deals with them. We make no distinction between terrorists and those who knowingly harbor or provide aid to them.

The struggle against global terrorism is different from any other war in our history. It will be fought on many fronts against a particularly elusive enemy over an extended period of time. Progress will come through the persistent accumulation of successes—some seen, some unseen.

Today our enemies have seen the results of what civilized nations can, and will, do against regimes that harbor, support, and use terrorism to achieve their political goals. Afghanistan has been liberated; coalition forces continue to hunt down the Taliban and al-Qaeda. But it is not only this battlefield on which we will engage terrorists. Thousands of trained terrorists remain at large with cells in North America, South America, Europe, Africa, the Middle East, and across Asia.

Our priority will be first to disrupt and destroy terrorist organizations of global reach and attack their leadership; command, control, and communications; material support; and finances. This will have a disabling effect upon the terrorists' ability to plan and operate.

We will continue to encourage our regional partners to take up a coordinated effort that isolates the terrorists. Once the regional campaign localizes the threat to a particular state, we will help ensure the state has the military, law enforcement, political, and financial tools necessary to finish the task.

The United States will continue to work with our allies to disrupt the financing of terrorism. We will identify and block the sources of funding for terrorism, freeze the assets of terrorists and those who support them, deny terrorists access to the international financial system, protect legitimate charities from being abused by terrorists, and prevent the movement of terrorists' assets through alternative financial networks.

However, this campaign need not be sequential to be effective, the cumulative effect across all regions will help achieve the results we seek. We will disrupt and destroy terrorist organizations by:

- direct and continuous action using all the elements of national and international power. Our immediate focus will be those terrorist organizations of global reach and any terrorist or state sponsor of terrorism which attempts to gain or use weapons of mass destruction (WMD) or their precursors;
- defending the United States, the American people, and our interests at home and abroad by identifying and destroying the threat before it reaches our borders. While the United States will constantly strive to enlist the support of the international community, we will not hesitate to act alone, if necessary, to exercise our right of self defense by acting preemptively against such terrorists, to prevent them from doing harm against our people and our country; and
- denying further sponsorship, support, and sanctuary to terrorists by convincing or compelling states to accept their sovereign responsibilities. We will also wage a war of ideas to win the battle against international terrorism. This includes:
- using the full influence of the United States, and working closely with allies and friends, to make clear that all acts of terrorism are illegitimate so that terrorism will be viewed in the same light as slavery, piracy, or genocide: behavior that no respectable government can condone or support and all must oppose;
- supporting moderate and modern government, especially in the Muslim world, to ensure that the conditions and ideologies that promote terrorism do not find fertile ground in any nation;
- diminishing the underlying conditions that spawn terrorism by enlisting the international community to focus its efforts and resources on areas most at risk; and
- using effective public diplomacy to promote the free flow of information and ideas to kindle the hopes and aspirations of freedom of those in societies ruled by the sponsors of global terrorism.

While we recognize that our best defense is a good offense, we are also strengthening America's homeland security to protect against and deter attack. This Administration has proposed the largest government reorganization since the Truman Administration created the National Security Council and the Department of Defense. Centered on a new Department of Homeland Security and including a new unified military command and a fundamental reordering of the FBI, our comprehensive plan to secure the homeland encompasses every level of government and the cooperation of the public and the private sector.

This strategy will turn adversity into opportunity. For example, emergency management systems will be better able to cope not just with terrorism but with all hazards. Our medical system will be strengthened to manage not just bioterror, but all infectious diseases and mass-casualty dangers. Our border controls will not just stop terrorists, but improve the efficient movement of legitimate traffic.

While our focus is protecting America, we know that to defeat terrorism in today's globalized world we need support from our allies and friends. Wherever possible, the United States will rely on regional organizations and state powers to meet their obligations to fight terrorism. Where governments find the fight against terrorism beyond their capacities, we will match their willpower and their resources with whatever help we and our allies can provide.

As we pursue the terrorists in Afghanistan, we will continue to work with international organizations such as the United Nations, as well as non-governmental organizations, and other countries to provide the humanitarian, political, economic, and security assistance necessary to rebuild Afghanistan so that it will never again abuse its people, threaten its neighbors, and provide a haven for terrorists.

In the war against global terrorism, we will never forget that we are ultimately fighting for our democratic values and way of life. Freedom and fear are at war, and there will be no quick or easy end to this conflict. In leading the campaign against terrorism, we are forging new, productive international relationships and redefining existing ones in ways that meet the challenges of the twenty-first century.

IV. WORK WITH OTHERS
TO DEFUSE REGIONAL CONFLICTS

"We build a world of justice, or we will live in a world of coercion. The magnitude of our shared responsibilities makes our disagreements look so small."

President George W. Bush
Berlin, Germany
May 23, 2002

Concerned nations must remain actively engaged in critical regional disputes to avoid explosive escalation and minimize human suffering. In an increasingly interconnected world, regional crisis can strain our alliances, rekindle rivalries among the major powers, and create horrifying affronts to human dignity. When violence erupts and states falter, the United States will work with friends and partners to alleviate suffering and restore stability.

No doctrine can anticipate every circumstance in which U.S. action—direct or indirect—is warranted. We have finite political, economic, and military resources to meet our global priorities. The United States will approach each case with these strategic principles in mind:

- The United States should invest time and resources into building international relationships and institutions that can help manage local crises when they emerge.
- The United States should be realistic about its ability to help those who are unwilling or unready to help themselves. Where and when people are ready to do their part, we will be willing to move decisively.

The Israeli–Palestinian conflict is critical because of the toll of human suffering, because of America's close relationship with the state of Israel and key Arab states, and because of that region's importance to other global priorities of the United States. There can be no peace for either side without freedom for both sides. America stands committed to an independent and democratic Palestine, living beside Israel in peace and security. Like all other people, Palestinians deserve a government that serves their interests and listens to their voices. The United States will continue to encourage all parties to step up to their responsibilities as we seek a just and comprehensive settlement to the conflict.

The United States, the international donor community, and the World Bank stand ready to work with a reformed Palestinian government on economic development, increased humanitarian assistance, and a program to establish, finance, and monitor a truly independent judiciary. If Palestinians embrace democracy, and the rule of law, confront corruption, and firmly reject terror, they can count on American support for the creation of a Palestinian state.

Israel also has a large stake in the success of a democratic Palestine. Permanent occupation threatens Israel's identity and democracy. So the United States continues to challenge Israeli leaders to take concrete steps to support the emergence of a viable, credible Palestinian state. As there is progress towards security, Israel forces need to withdraw fully to positions they held prior to September 28, 2000. And consistent with the recommendations of the Mitchell Committee, Israeli settlement activity in the occupied territories must stop. As violence subsides, freedom of movement should be restored, permitting innocent Palestinians to resume work and normal life. The United States can play a crucial role but, ultimately, lasting peace can only come when Israelis and Palestinians resolve the issues and end the conflict between them.

In South Asia, the United States has also emphasized the need for India and Pakistan to resolve their disputes. This Administration invested time and resources building strong bilateral relations with India and Pakistan. These strong relations then gave us leverage to play a constructive role when tensions in the region became acute. With Pakistan, our bilateral relations have been bolstered by Pakistan's choice to join the war against terror and move toward building a more open and tolerant society. The Administration sees India's potential to become one of the great democratic powers of the twenty-first century and has worked hard to transform our relationship accordingly. Our involvement in this regional dispute, building on earlier investments in bilateral relations, looks first to concrete steps by India and Pakistan that can help defuse military confrontation.

Indonesia took courageous steps to create a working democracy and respect for the rule of law. By tolerating ethnic minorities, respecting the rule of law, and accepting open markets, Indonesia may be able to employ the engine of opportunity that has helped lift some of its neighbors out of poverty and desperation. It is the initiative by Indonesia that allows U.S. assistance to make a difference.

In the Western Hemisphere we have formed flexible coalitions with countries that share our priorities, particularly Mexico, Brazil, Canada, Chile, and Colombia. Together we will promote a truly democratic hemisphere where our integration advances security, prosperity, opportunity, and hope. We will work with regional institutions, such as the Summit of the Americas process, the Organization of American States (OAS), and the Defense Ministerial of the Americas for the benefit of the entire hemisphere.

Parts of Latin America confront regional conflict, especially arising from the violence of drug cartels and their accomplices. This conflict and unrestrained narcotics trafficking could imperil the health and security of the United States. Therefore we have developed an active strategy to help the Andean nations adjust their economies, enforce their laws, defeat terrorist organizations, and cut off the supply of drugs, while—as important—we work to reduce the demand for drugs in our own country.

In Colombia, we recognize the link between terrorist and extremist groups that challenge the security of the state and drug trafficking activities that help finance the operations of such groups. We are working to help Colombia defend its democratic institutions and defeat illegal armed groups of both the left and right by extending effective sovereignty over the entire national territory and provide basic security to the Colombian people.

In Africa, promise and opportunity sit side by side with disease, war, and desperate poverty. This threatens both a core value of the United States— preserving human dignity—and our strategic priority—combating global terror. American interests and American principles, therefore, lead in the same direction: we will work with others for an African continent that lives in liberty, peace, and growing prosperity. Together with our European allies, we must help strengthen Africa's fragile states, help build indigenous capability to secure porous borders, and help build up the law enforcement and intelligence infrastructure to deny havens for terrorists.

An ever more lethal environment exists in Africa as local civil wars spread beyond borders to create regional war zones. Forming coalitions of the willing and cooperative security arrangements are key to confronting these emerging transnational threats.

Africa's great size and diversity requires a security strategy that focuses on bilateral engagement and builds coalitions of the willing. This Administration will focus on three interlocking strategies for the region:

- countries with major impact on their neighborhood such as South Africa, Nigeria, Kenya, and Ethiopia are anchors for regional engagement and require focused attention;
- coordination with European allies and international institutions is essential for constructive conflict mediation and successful peace operations; and
- Africa's capable reforming states and sub-regional organizations must be strengthened as the primary means to address transnational threats on a sustained basis.

Ultimately the path of political and economic freedom presents the surest route to progress in sub-Saharan Africa, where most wars are conflicts over material resources and political access often tragically waged on the basis of ethnic and religious difference. The transition to the African Union with its stated commitment to good governance and a common responsibility for democratic political systems offers opportunities to strengthen democracy on the continent.

V. PREVENT OUR ENEMIES FROM THREATENING US, OUR ALLIES, AND OUR FRIENDS WITH WEAPONS OF MASS DESTRUCTION

"The gravest danger to freedom lies at the crossroads of radicalism and technology. When the spread of chemical and biological and nuclear weapons, along with ballistic missile technology—when that occurs, even weak states and small groups could attain a catastrophic power to strike great nations. Our enemies have declared this very intention, and have been caught seeking these terrible weapons. They want the capability to blackmail us, or to harm us, or to harm our friends—and we will oppose them with all our power."

President George W. Bush
West Point, New York
June 1, 2002

The nature of the Cold War threat required the United States—with our allies and friends—to emphasize deterrence of the enemy's use of force, producing a grim strategy of mutual assured destruction. With the collapse of the Soviet Union and the end of the Cold War, our security environment has undergone profound transformation.

Having moved from confrontation to cooperation as the hallmark of our relationship with Russia, the dividends are evident: an end to the balance of terror that divided us; an historic reduction in the nuclear arsenals on both sides; and cooperation in areas such as counterterrorism and missile defense that until recently were inconceivable.

But new deadly challenges have emerged from rogue states and terrorists. None of these contemporary threats rival the sheer destructive power that was arrayed against us by the Soviet Union. However, the nature and motivations of these new adversaries, their determination to obtain destructive powers hitherto available only to the world's strongest states, and the greater likelihood that they will use weapons of mass destruction against us, make today's security environment more complex and dangerous.

In the 1990s we witnessed the emergence of a small number of rogue states that, while different in important ways, share a number of attributes. These states:

- brutalize their own people and squander their national resources for the personal gain of the rulers;
- display no regard for international law, threaten their neighbors, and callously violate international treaties to which they are party;
- are determined to acquire weapons of mass destruction, along with other advanced military technology, to be used as threats or offensively to achieve the aggressive designs of these regimes;
- sponsor terrorism around the globe; and reject basic human values and hate the United States and everything for which it stands.

At the time of the Gulf War, we acquired irrefutable proof that Iraq's designs were not limited to the chemical weapons it had used against Iran and its own people, but also extended to the acquisition of nuclear weapons and biological agents. In the past decade North Korea has become the world's principal purveyor of ballistic missiles, and has tested increasingly capable missiles while developing its own WMD arsenal. Other rogue regimes seek nuclear, biological, and chemical weapons as well. These states' pursuit of, and global trade in, such weapons has become a looming threat to all nations.

We must be prepared to stop rogue states and their terrorist clients before they are able to threaten or use weapons of mass destruction against the United States and our allies and friends. Our response must take full advantage of strengthened alliances, the establishment of new partnerships with former adversaries, innovation in the use of military forces, modern technologies, including the development of an effective missile defense system, and increased emphasis on intelligence collection and analysis.

Our comprehensive strategy to combat WMD includes:

- *Proactive counterproliferation efforts.* We must deter and defend against the threat before it is unleashed. We must ensure that key capabilities— detection, active and passive defenses, and counterforce capabilities— are integrated into our defense transformation and our homeland security systems. Counterproliferation must also be integrated into the doctrine, training, and equipping of our forces and those of our allies to ensure that we can prevail in any conflict with WMD-armed adversaries.

- *Strengthened nonproliferation efforts to prevent rogue states and terrorists from acquiring the materials, technologies, and expertise necessary for weapons of mass destruction.* We will enhance diplomacy, arms control, multilateral export controls, and threat reduction assistance that impede states and terrorists seeking WMD, and when necessary, interdict enabling technologies and materials. We will continue to build coalitions to support these efforts, encouraging their increased political and financial support for nonproliferation and threat reduction programs. The recent G-8 agreement to commit up to $20 billion to a global partnership against proliferation marks a major step forward.

- *Effective consequence management to respond to the effects of WMD use, whether by terrorists or hostile states.* Minimizing the effects of WMD use against our people will help deter those who possess such weapons and dissuade those who seek to acquire them by persuading enemies that they cannot attain their desired ends. The United States must also be prepared to respond to the effects of WMD use against our forces abroad, and to help friends and allies if they are attacked.

It has taken almost a decade for us to comprehend the true nature of this new threat. Given the goals of rogue states and terrorists, the United States can no longer solely rely on a reactive posture as we have in the past. The inability to deter a potential attacker, the immediacy of today's threats, and the magnitude of potential harm that could be caused by our adversaries' choice of weapons, do not permit that option. We cannot let our enemies strike first.

In the Cold War, especially following the Cuban missile crisis, we faced a generally status quo, risk-averse adversary. Deterrence was an effective defense. But deterrence based only upon the threat of retaliation is less likely to work against leaders of rogue states more willing to take risks, gambling with the lives of their people, and the wealth of their nations.

- In the Cold War, weapons of mass destruction were considered weapons of last resort whose use risked the destruction of those who used them. Today, our enemies see weapons of mass destruction as weapons of choice. For rogue states these weapons are tools of intimidation and military aggression against their neighbors. These weapons may also allow these states to attempt to blackmail the United States and our allies to prevent us from deterring or repelling the aggressive behavior of rogue states. Such states also see these weapons as their best means of overcoming the conventional superiority of the United States.
- Traditional concepts of deterrence will not work against a terrorist enemy whose avowed tactics are wanton destruction and the targeting of innocents; whose so-called soldiers seek martyrdom in death and whose most potent protection is statelessness. The overlap between states that sponsor terror and those that pursue WMD compels us to action.

For centuries, international law recognized that nations need not suffer an attack before they can lawfully take action to defend themselves against forces that present an imminent danger of attack. Legal scholars and international jurists often conditioned the legitimacy of preemption on the existence of an imminent threat—most often a visible mobilization of armies, navies, and air forces preparing to attack.

We must adapt the concept of imminent threat to the capabilities and objectives of today's adversaries. Rogue states and terrorists do not seek to attack us using conventional means. They know such attacks would fail. Instead, they rely on acts of terror and, potentially, the use of weapons of mass destruction—weapons that can be easily concealed, delivered covertly, and used without warning.

The targets of these attacks are our military forces and our civilian population, in direct violation of one of the principal norms of the law of warfare.

As was demonstrated by the losses on September 11, 2001, mass civilian casualties is the specific objective of terrorists and these losses would be exponentially more severe if terrorists acquired and used weapons of mass destruction.

The United States has long maintained the option of preemptive actions to counter a sufficient threat to our national security. The greater the threat, the greater is the risk of inaction—and the more compelling the case for taking anticipatory action to defend ourselves, even if uncertainty remains as to the time and place of the enemy's attack. To forestall or prevent such hostile acts by our adversaries, the United States will, if necessary, act preemptively.

The United States will not use force in all cases to preempt emerging threats, nor should nations use preemption as a pretext for aggression. Yet in an age where the enemies of civilization openly and actively seek the world's most destructive technologies, the United States cannot remain idle while dangers gather. We will always proceed deliberately, weighing the consequences of our actions. To support preemptive options, we will:

- build better, more integrated intelligence capabilities to provide timely, accurate information on threats, wherever they may emerge;
- coordinate closely with allies to form a common assessment of the most dangerous threats; and
- continue to transform our military forces to ensure our ability to conduct rapid and precise operations to achieve decisive results.

The purpose of our actions will always be to eliminate a specific threat to the United States or our allies and friends. The reasons for our actions will be clear, the force measured, and the cause just.

VI. IGNITE A NEW ERA OF GLOBAL ECONOMIC GROWTH THROUGH FREE MARKETS AND FREE TRADE

"When nations close their markets and opportunity is hoarded by a privileged few, no amount-no amount-of development aid is ever enough. When nations respect their people, open markets, invest in better health and education, every dollar of aid, every dollar of trade revenue and domestic capital is used more effectively."

President George W. Bush
Monterrey, Mexico
March 22, 2002

A strong world economy enhances our national security by advancing prosperity and freedom in the rest of the world. Economic growth supported by free trade and free markets creates new jobs and higher incomes. It allows people to lift their lives out of poverty, spurs economic and legal reform, and the fight against corruption, and it reinforces the habits of liberty.

We will promote economic growth and economic freedom beyond America's shores. All governments are responsible for creating their own economic policies and responding to their own economic challenges. We will use our economic engagement with other countries to underscore the benefits of policies that generate higher productivity and sustained economic growth, including:

- pro-growth legal and regulatory policies to encourage business investment, innovation, and entrepreneurial activity;
- tax policies—particularly lower marginal tax rates—that improve incentives for work and investment;
- rule of law and intolerance of corruption so that people are confident that they will be able to enjoy the fruits of their economic endeavors;
- strong financial systems that allow capital to be put to its most efficient use;
- sound fiscal policies to support business activity;
- investments in health and education that improve the well-being and skills of the labor force and population as a whole; and
- free trade that provides new avenues for growth and fosters the diffusion of technologies and ideas that increase productivity and opportunity.

The lessons of history are clear: market economies, not command-and-control economies with the heavy hand of government, are the best way to promote prosperity and reduce poverty. Policies that further strengthen market incentives and market institutions are relevant for all economies—industrialized countries, emerging markets, and the developing world.

A return to strong economic growth in Europe and Japan is vital to U.S. national security interests. We want our allies to have strong economies for their own sake, for the sake of the global economy, and for the sake of global security. European efforts to remove structural barriers in their economies are particularly important in this regard, as are Japan's efforts to end deflation and address the problems of non-performing loans in the Japanese banking system. We will continue to use our regular consultations with Japan and our European partners—including through the Group of Seven (G-7)—to discuss policies they are adopting to promote growth in their economies and support higher global economic growth.

Improving stability in emerging markets is also key to global economic growth. International flows of investment capital are needed to expand the productive potential of these economies. These flows allow emerging markets and developing countries to make the investments that raise living standards and reduce poverty. Our long-term objective should be a world in which all countries have investment-grade credit ratings that allow them access to international capital markets and to invest in their future.

We are committed to policies that will help emerging markets achieve access to larger capital flows at lower cost. To this end, we will continue to pursue reforms aimed at reducing uncertainty in financial markets. We will work actively with other countries, the International Monetary Fund (IMF), and the private sector to implement the G-7 Action Plan negotiated earlier this year for preventing financial crises and more effectively resolving them when they occur.

The best way to deal with financial crises is to prevent them from occurring, and we have encouraged the IMF to improve its efforts doing so. We will continue to work with the IMF to streamline the policy conditions for its lending and to focus its lending strategy on achieving economic growth through sound fiscal and monetary policy, exchange rate policy, and financial sector policy.

The concept of "free trade" arose as a moral principle even before it became a pillar of economics. If you can make something that others value, you should be able to sell it to them. If others make something that you value, you should be able to buy it. This is real freedom, the freedom for a person—or a nation—to make a living. To promote free trade, the Unites States has developed a comprehensive strategy:

- *Seize the global initiative.* The new global trade negotiations we helped launch at Doha in November 2001 will have an ambitious agenda, especially in agriculture, manufacturing, and services, targeted for completion in 2005. The United States has led the way in completing the accession of China and a democratic Taiwan to the World Trade Organization. We will assist Russia's preparations to join the WTO.
- *Press regional initiatives.* The United States and other democracies in the Western Hemisphere have agreed to create the Free Trade Area of the Americas, targeted for completion in 2005. This year the United States will advocate market-access negotiations with its partners, targeted on agriculture, industrial goods, services, investment, and government procurement. We will also offer more opportunity to the poorest continent, Africa, starting with full use of the preferences allowed in the African Growth and Opportunity Act, and leading to free trade.
- *Move ahead with bilateral free trade agreements.* Building on the free trade agreement with Jordan enacted in 2001, the Administration will

work this year to complete free trade agreements with Chile and Singapore. Our aim is to achieve free trade agreements with a mix of developed and developing countries in all regions of the world. Initially, Central America, Southern Africa, Morocco, and Australia will be our principal focal points.

- *Renew the executive-congressional partnership.* Every administration's trade strategy depends on a productive partnership with Congress. After a gap of eight years, the Administration reestablished majority support in the Congress for trade liberalization by passing Trade Promotion Authority and the other market opening measures for developing countries in the Trade Act of 2002. This Administration will work with Congress to enact new bilateral, regional, and global trade agreements that will be concluded under the recently passed Trade Promotion Authority.

- *Promote the connection between trade and development.* Trade policies can help developing countries strengthen property rights, competition, the rule of law, investment, the spread of knowledge, open societies, the efficient allocation of resources, and regional integration—all leading to growth, opportunity, and confidence in developing countries. The United States is implementing The Africa Growth and Opportunity Act to provide market-access for nearly all goods produced in the thirty-five countries of sub-Saharan Africa. We will make more use of this act and its equivalent for the Caribbean Basin and continue to work with multilateral and regional institutions to help poorer countries take advantage of these opportunities. Beyond market access, the most important area where trade intersects with poverty is in public health. We will ensure that the WTO intellectual property rules are flexible enough to allow developing nations to gain access to critical medicines for extraordinary dangers like HIV/AIDS, tuberculosis, and malaria.

- *Enforce trade agreements and laws against unfair practices.* Commerce depends on the rule of law; international trade depends on enforceable agreements. Our top priorities are to resolve ongoing disputes with the European Union, Canada, and Mexico and to make a global effort to address new technology, science, and health regulations that needlessly impede farm exports and improved agriculture. Laws against unfair trade practices are often abused, but the international community must be able to address genuine concerns about government subsidies and dumping. International industrial espionage which undermines fair competition must be detected and deterred.

- *Help domestic industries and workers adjust.* There is a sound statutory framework for these transitional safeguards which we have used in the agricultural sector and which we are using this year to help the American steel industry. The benefits of free trade depend upon the enforcement of fair trading practices. These safeguards help ensure that the benefits of free trade do not come at the expense of American workers. Trade adjustment assistance will help workers adapt to the change and dynamism of open markets.

- *Protect the environment and workers.* The United States must foster economic growth in ways that will provide a better life along with widening prosperity. We will incorporate labor and .environmental concerns into U.S. trade negotiations, creating a healthy "network" between multilateral environmental agreements with the WTO, and use the International Labor Organization, trade preference programs, and trade talks to improve working conditions in conjunction with freer trade.
- *Enhance energy security.* We will strengthen our own energy security and the shared prosperity of the global economy by working with our allies, trading partners, and energy producers to expand the sources and types of global energy supplied, especially in the Western Hemisphere, Africa, Central Asia, and the Caspian region. We will also continue to work with our partners to develop cleaner and more energy efficient technologies.

Economic growth should be accompanied by global efforts to stabilize greenhouse gas concentrations associated with this growth, containing them at a level that prevents dangerous human interference with the global climate. Our overall objective is to reduce America's greenhouse gas emissions relative to the size of our economy, cutting such emissions per unit of economic activity by 18 percent over the next ten years, by the year 2012. Our strategies for attaining this goal will be to:

- remain committed to the basic U.N. Framework Convention for international cooperation;
- obtain agreements with key industries to cut emissions of some of the most potent greenhouse gases and give transferable credits to companies that can show real cuts;
- develop improved standards for measuring and registering emission reductions;
- promote renewable energy production and clean coal technology, as well as nuclear power—which produces no greenhouse gas emissions, while also improving fuel economy for U.S. cars and trucks;
- increase spending on research and new conservation technologies, to a total of $4.5 billion—the largest sum being spent on climate change by any country in the world and a $700 million increase over last year's budget; and

- assist developing countries, especially the major greenhouse gas emitters such as China and India, so that they will have the tools and resources to join this effort and be able to grow along a cleaner and better path.

VII. EXPAND THE CIRCLE OF DEVELOPMENT BY OPENING SOCIETIES AND BUILDING THE INFRASTRUCTURE OF DEMOCRACY

"In World War II we fought to make the world safer, then worked to rebuild it. As we wage war today to keep the world safe from terror, we must also work to make the world a better place for all its citizens."

President George W. Bush
Washington, D.C. (Inter-American Development Bank)
March 14, 2002

A world where some live in comfort and plenty, while half of the human race lives on less than two dollars a day, is neither just nor stable. Including all of the world's poor in an expanding circle of development—and opportunity—is a moral imperative and one of the top priorities of U.S. international policy.

Decades of massive development assistance have failed to spur economic growth in the poorest countries. Worse, development aid has often served to prop up failed policies, relieving the pressure for reform and perpetuating misery. Results of aid are typically measured in dollars spent by donors, not in the rates of growth and poverty reduction achieved by recipients. These are the indicators of a failed strategy.

Working with other nations, the United States is confronting this failure. We forged a new consensus at the U.N. Conference on Financing for Development in Monterrey that the objectives of assistance—and the strategies to achieve those objectives—must change.

This Administration's goal is to help unleash the productive potential of individuals in all nations. Sustained growth and poverty reduction is impossible without the right national policies. Where governments have implemented real policy changes, we will provide significant new levels of assistance. The United States and other developed countries should set an ambitious and specific target: to double the size of the world's poorest economies within a decade.

The United States Government will pursue these major strategies to achieve this goal:

- *Provide resources to aid countries that have met the challenge of national reform.* We propose a 50 percent increase in the core development assistance given by the United States. While continuing our present programs, including humanitarian assistance based on need alone, these billions of new dollars will form a new Millennium Challenge Account for projects in countries whose governments rule justly, invest in their people, and encourage economic freedom. Governments must fight corruption, respect basic human rights, embrace the rule of law, invest in health care and education, follow responsible economic policies, and enable entrepreneurship. The Millennium Challenge Account will reward countries that have demonstrated real policy change and challenge those that have not to implement reforms.

- *Improve the effectiveness of the World Bank and other development banks in raising living standards.* The United States is committed to a comprehensive reform agenda for making the World Bank and the other multilateral development banks more effective in improving the lives of the world's poor. We have reversed the downward trend in U.S. contributions and proposed an 18 percent increase in the U.S. contributions to the International Development Association (IDA)—the World Bank's fund for the poorest countries—and the African Development Fund. The key to raising living standards and reducing poverty around the world is increasing productivity growth, especially in the poorest countries. We will continue to press the multilateral development banks to focus on activities that increase economic productivity, such as improvements in education, health, rule of law, and private sector development. Every project, every loan, every grant must be judged by how much it will increase productivity growth in developing countries.
- *Insist upon measurable results to ensure that development assistance is actually making a difference in the lives of the world's poor.* When it comes to economic development, what really matters is that more children are getting a better education, more people have access to health care and clean water, or more workers can find jobs to make a better future for their families. We have a moral obligation to measure the success of our development assistance by whether it is delivering results. For this reason, we will continue to demand that our own development assistance as well as assistance from the multilateral development banks has measurable goals and concrete benchmarks for achieving those goals. Thanks to U.S. leadership, the recent IDA replenishment agreement will establish a monitoring and evaluation system that measures recipient countries' progress. For the first time, donors can link a portion of their contributions to IDA to the achievement of actual development results, and part of the U.S. contribution is linked in this way. We will strive to make sure that the World Bank and other multilateral development banks

build on this progress so that a focus on results is an integral part of everything that these institutions do.

- *Increase the amount of development assistance that is provided in the form of grants instead of loans.* Greater use of results-based grants is the best way to help poor countries make productive investments, particularly in the social sectors, without saddling them with ever-larger debt burdens. As a result of U.S. leadership, the recent IDA agreement provided for significant increases in grant funding for the poorest countries for education, HIV/AIDS, health, nutrition, water, sanitation, and other human needs. Our goal is to build on that progress by increasing the use of grants at the other multilateral development banks. We will also challenge universities, nonprofits, and the private sector to match government efforts by using grants to support development projects that show results.
- *Open societies to commerce and investment. Trade and investment are the real engines of economic growth.* Even if government aid increases, most money for development must come from trade, domestic capital, and foreign investment. An effective strategy must try to expand these flows as well. Free markets and free trade are key priorities of our national security strategy.
- *Secure public health.* The scale of the public health crisis in poor countries is enormous. In countries afflicted by epidemics and pandemics like HIV/AIDS, malaria, and tuberculosis, growth and development will be threatened until these scourges can be contained. Resources from the developed world are necessary but will be effective only with honest governance, which supports prevention programs and provides effective local infrastructure. The United States has strongly backed the new global fund for HIV/AIDS organized by U.N. Secretary General Kofi Annan and its focus on combining prevention with a broad strategy for treatment and care. The United States already contributes more than twice as much money to such efforts as the next largest donor. If the global fund demonstrates its promise, we will be ready to give even more.
- *Emphasize education.* Literacy and learning are the foundation of democracy and development. Only about 7 percent of World Bank resources are devoted to education. This proportion should grow. The United States will increase its own funding for education assistance by at least 20 percent with an emphasis on improving basic education and teacher training in Africa. The United States can also bring information technology to these societies, many of whose education systems have been devastated by HIV/AIDS.
- *Continue to aid agricultural development.* New technologies, including biotechnology, have enormous potential to improve crop yields in

developing countries while using fewer pesticides and less water. Using sound science, the United States should help bring these benefits to the 800 million people, including 300 million children, who still suffer from hunger and malnutrition.

VIII. DEVELOP AGENDAS FOR COOPERATIVE ACTION WITH THE OTHER MAIN CENTERS OF GLOBAL POWER

"We have our best chance since the rise of the nation–state in the seventeenth century to build a world where the great powers compete in peace instead of prepare for war."

President George W. Bush
West Point, New York
June 1, 2002

America will implement its strategies by organizing coalitions—as broad as practicable—of states able and willing to promote a balance of power that favors freedom. Effective coalition leadership requires clear priorities, an appreciation of others' interests, and consistent consultations among partners with a spirit of humility.

There is little of lasting consequence that the United States can accomplish in the world without the sustained cooperation of its allies and friends in Canada and Europe. Europe is also the seat of two of the strongest and most able international institutions in the world: the North Atlantic Treaty Organization (NATO), which has, since its inception, been the fulcrum of transatlantic and inter-European security, and the European Union (EU), our partner in opening world trade.

The attacks of September 11 were also an attack on NATO, as NATO itself recognized when it invoked its Article V self-defense clause for the first time. NATO's core mission—collective defense of the transatlantic alliance of democracies—remains, but NATO must develop new structures and capabilities to carry out that mission under new circumstances. NATO must build a capability to field, at short notice, highly mobile, specially trained forces whenever they are needed to respond to a threat against any member of the alliance.

The alliance must be able to act wherever our interests are threatened, creating coalitions under NATO's own mandate, as well as contributing to mission-based coalitions. To achieve this, we must:

- expand NATO's membership to those democratic nations willing and able to share the burden of defending and advancing our common interests;

- ensure that the military forces of NATO nations have appropriate combat contributions to make in coalition warfare;
- develop planning processes to enable those contributions to become effective multinational fighting forces;
- take advantage of the technological opportunities and economies of scale in our defense spending to transform NATO military forces so that they dominate potential aggressors and diminish our vulnerabilities;
- streamline and increase the flexibility of command structures to meet new operational demands and the associated requirements of training, integrating, and experimenting with new force configurations; and
- maintain the ability to work and fight together as allies even as we take the necessary steps to transform and modernize our forces.

If NATO succeeds in enacting these changes, the rewards will be a partnership as central to the security and interests of its member states as was the case during the Cold War. We will sustain a common perspective on the threats to our societies and improve our ability to take common action in defense of our nations and their interests. At the same time, we welcome our European allies' efforts to forge a greater foreign policy and defense identity with the EU, and commit ourselves to close consultations to ensure that these developments work with NATO. We cannot afford to lose this opportunity to better prepare the family of transatlantic democracies for the challenges to come.

The attacks of September 11 energized America's Asian alliances. Australia invoked the ANZUS Treaty to declare the September 11 was an attack on Australia itself, following that historic decision with the dispatch of some of the world's finest combat forces for Operation Enduring Freedom. Japan and the Republic of Korea provided unprecedented levels of military logistical support within weeks of the terrorist attack. We have deepened cooperation on counterterrorism with our alliance partners in Thailand and the Philippines and received invaluable assistance from close friends like Singapore and New Zealand.

The war against terrorism has proven that America's alliances in Asia not only underpin regional peace and stability, but are flexible and ready to deal with new challenges. To enhance our Asian alliances and friendships, we will:

- look to Japan to continue forging a leading role in regional and global affairs based on our common interests, our common values, and our close defense and diplomatic cooperation;
- work with South Korea to maintain vigilance towards the North while preparing our alliance to make contributions to the broader stability of the region over the longer term;

- build on fifty years of U.S.–Australian alliance cooperation as we continue working together to resolve regional and global problems—as we have so many times from the Battle of the Coral Sea to Tora Bora;
- maintain forces in the region that reflect our commitments to our allies, our requirements, our technological advances, and the strategic environment; and
- build on stability provided by these alliances, as well as with institutions such as ASEAN and the Asia–Pacific Economic Cooperation forum, to develop a mix of regional and bilateral strategies to manage change in this dynamic region.

We are attentive to the possible renewal of old patterns of great power competition. Several potential great powers are now in the midst of internal transition—most importantly Russia, India, and China. In all three cases, recent developments have encouraged our hope that a truly global consensus about basic principles is slowly taking shape.

With Russia, we are already building a new strategic relationship based on a central reality of the twenty-first century: the United States and Russia are no longer strategic adversaries. The Moscow Treaty on Strategic Reductions is emblematic of this new reality and reflects a critical change in Russian thinking that promises to lead to productive, long-term relations with the Euro-Atlantic community and the United States. Russia's top leaders have a realistic assessment of their country's current weakness and the policies—internal and external—needed to reverse those weaknesses. They understand, increasingly, that Cold War approaches do not serve their national interests and that Russian and American strategic interests overlap in many areas.

United States policy seeks to use this turn in Russian thinking to refocus our relationship on emerging and potential common interests and challenges. We are broadening our already extensive cooperation in the global war on terrorism. We are facilitating Russia's entry into the World Trade Organization, without lowering standards for accession, to promote beneficial bilateral trade and investment relations. We have created the NATO–Russia Council with the goal of deepening security cooperation among Russia, our European allies, and ourselves. We will continue to bolster the independence and stability of the states of the former Soviet Union in the belief that a prosperous and stable neighborhood will reinforce Russia's growing commitment to integration into the Euro-Atlantic community.

At the same time, we are realistic about the differences that still divide us from Russia and about the time and effort it will take to build an enduring strategic partnership. Lingering distrust of our motives and policies by key Russian elites slows improvement in our relations. Russia's uneven commitment to the basic values of free-market democracy and dubious record in combating the proliferation of weapons of mass destruction remain matters of great concern. Russia's very weakness limits the opportunities for cooperation. Nevertheless, those opportunities are vastly greater now than in recent years—or even decades.

The United States has undertaken a transformation in its bilateral relationship with India based on a conviction that U.S. interests require a strong relationship with India. We are the two largest democracies, committed to political freedom protected by representative government. India is moving toward greater economic freedom as well. We have a common interest in the free flow of commerce, including through the vital sea lanes of the Indian Ocean. Finally, we share an interest in fighting terrorism and in creating a strategically stable Asia.

Differences remain, including over the development of India's nuclear and missile programs, and the pace of India's economic reforms. But while in the past these concerns may have dominated our thinking about India, today we start with a view of India as a growing world power with which we have common strategic interests. Through a strong partnership with India, we can best address any differences and shape a dynamic future.

The United States relationship with China is an important part of our strategy to promote a stable, peaceful, and prosperous Asia-Pacific region. We welcome the emergence of a strong, peaceful, and prosperous China. The democratic development of China is crucial to that future. Yet, a quarter century after beginning the process of shedding the worst features of the Communist legacy, China's leaders have not yet made the next series of fundamental choices about the character of their state. In pursuing advanced military capabilities that can threaten its neighbors in the Asia-Pacific region, China is following an outdated path that, in the end, will hamper its own pursuit of national greatness. In time, China will find that social and political freedom is the only source of that greatness.

The United States seeks a constructive relationship with a changing China. We already cooperate well where our interests overlap, including the current war on terrorism and in promoting stability on the Korean peninsula. Likewise, we have coordinated on the future of Afghanistan and have initiated a comprehensive dialogue on counterterrorism and similar transitional concerns. Shared health and environmental threats, such as the spread of HIV/AIDS, challenge us to promote jointly the welfare of our citizens.

Addressing these transnational threats will challenge China to become more open with information, promote the development of civil society, and enhance individual human rights. China has begun to take the road to political openness, permitting many personal freedoms and conducting village-level elections, yet remains strongly committed to national one-party rule by the Communist Party. To make that nation truly accountable to its citizen's needs and aspirations, however, much work remains to be done. Only by allowing the Chinese people to think, assemble, and worship freely can China reach its full potential.

Our important trade relationship will benefit from China's entry into the World Trade Organization, which will create more export opportunities and ultimately more jobs for American farmers, workers, and companies. China is our fourth largest trading partner, with over $100 billion in annual two-way trade. The power of market principles and the WTO's requirements for transparency and accountability will advance openness and the rule of law in China to help establish basic protections for commerce and for citizens. There are, however, other areas in which we have profound disagreements. Our commitment to the self-defense of Taiwan under the Taiwan Relations Act is one. Human rights is another. We expect China to adhere to its nonproliferation commitments. We will work to narrow differences where they exist, but not allow them to preclude cooperation where we agree.

The events of September 11, 2001, fundamentally changed the context for relations between the United States and other main centers of global power, and opened vast, new opportunities. With our long-standing allies in Europe and Asia, and with leaders in Russia, India, and China, we must develop active agendas of cooperation lest these relationships become routine and unproductive.

Every agency of the United States Government shares the challenge. We can build fruitful habits of consultation, quiet argument, sober analysis, and common action. In the long term, these are the practices that will sustain the supremacy of our common principles and keep open the path of progress.

IX. TRANSFORM AMERICA'S NATIONAL SECURITY INSTITUTIONS TO MEET THE CHALLENGES AND OPPORTUNITIES OF THE TWENTY-FIRST CENTURY

"Terrorists attacked a symbol of American prosperity. They did not touch its source. America is successful because of the hard work, creativity, and enterprise of our people."

President George W. Bush
Washington, D.C. (Joint Session of Congress)
September 20, 2001

The major institutions of American national security were designed in a different era to meet different requirements. All of them must be transformed.

It is time to reaffirm the essential role of American military strength. We must build and maintain our defenses beyond challenge. Our military's highest priority is to defend the United States. To do so effectively, our military must:

- assure our allies and friends;
- dissuade future military competition;
- deter threats against U.S. interests, allies, and friends; and
- decisively defeat any adversary if deterrence fails.

The unparalleled strength of the United States armed forces, and their forward presence, have maintained the peace in some of the world's most strategically vital regions. However, the threats and enemies we must confront have changed, and so must our forces. A military structured to deter massive Cold War–era armies must be transformed to focus more on how an adversary might fight rather than where and when a war might occur. We will channel our energies to overcome a host of operational challenges.

The presence of American forces overseas is one of the most profound symbols of the U.S. commitments to allies and friends. Through our willingness to use force in our own defense and in defense of others, the United States demonstrates its resolve to maintain a balance of power that favors freedom. To contend with uncertainty and to meet the many security challenges we face, the United States will require bases and stations within and beyond Western Europe and Northeast Asia, as well as temporary access arrangements for the long-distance deployment of U.S. forces.

Before the war in Afghanistan, that area was low on the list of major planning contingencies. Yet, in a very short time, we had to operate across the length and breadth of that remote nation, using every branch of the armed forces. We must prepare for more such deployments by developing assets such as advanced remote sensing, long-range precision strike capabilities, and transformed maneuver and expeditionary forces. This broad portfolio of military capabilities must also include the ability to defend the homeland, conduct information operations, ensure U.S. access to distant theaters, and protect critical U.S. infrastructure and assets in outer space.

Innovation within the armed forces will rest on experimentation with new approaches to warfare, strengthening joint operations, exploiting U.S. intelligence advantages, and taking full advantage of science and technology. We must also transform the way the Department of Defense is run, especially in financial management and recruitment and retention. Finally, while maintaining near-term readiness and the ability to fight the war on terrorism, the goal must be to provide the President with a wider range of military options to discourage aggression or any form of coercion against the United States, our allies, and our friends.

We know from history that deterrence can fail; and we know from experience that some enemies cannot be deterred. The United States must and will maintain the capability to defeat any attempt by an enemy—whether a state or non-state actor—to impose its will on the United States, our allies, or our friends. We will maintain the forces sufficient to support our obligations, and to defend freedom. Our forces will be strong enough to dissuade potential adversaries from pursuing a military build-up in hopes of surpassing, or equaling, the power of the United States.

Intelligence—and how we use it—is our first line of defense against terrorists and the threat posed by hostile states. Designed around the priority of gathering enormous information about a massive, fixed object—the Soviet bloc—the intelligence community is coping with the challenge of following a far more complex and elusive set of targets.

We must transform our intelligence capabilities and build new ones to keep pace with the nature of these threats. Intelligence must be appropriately integrated with our defense and law enforcement systems and coordinated with our allies and friends. We need to protect the capabilities we have so that we do not arm our enemies with the knowledge of how best to surprise us. Those who would harm us also seek the benefit of surprise to limit our prevention and response options and to maximize injury.

We must strengthen intelligence warning and analysis to provide integrated threat assessments for national and homeland security. Since the threats inspired by foreign governments and groups may be conducted inside the United States, we must also ensure the proper fusion of information between intelligence and law enforcement.

Initiatives in this area will include:

- strengthening the authority of the Director of Central Intelligence to lead the development and actions of the Nation's foreign intelligence capabilities;
- establishing a new framework for intelligence warning that provides seamless and integrated warning across the spectrum of threats facing the nation and our allies;
- continuing to develop new methods of collecting information to sustain our intelligence advantage;
- investing in future capabilities while working to protect them through a more vigorous effort to prevent the compromise of intelligence capabilities; and
- collecting intelligence against the terrorist danger across the government with allsource analysis.

As the United States Government relies on the armed forces to defend America's interests, it must rely on diplomacy to interact with other nations. We will ensure that the Department of State receives funding sufficient to ensure the success of American diplomacy. The State Department takes the lead in managing our bilateral relationships with other governments. And in this new era, its people and institutions must be able to interact equally adroitly with nongovernmental organizations and international institutions. Officials trained mainly in international politics must also extend their reach to understand complex issues of domestic governance around the world, including public health, education, law enforcement, the judiciary, and public diplomacy.

Our diplomats serve at the front line of complex negotiations, civil wars, and other humanitarian catastrophes. As humanitarian relief requirements are better understood, we must also be able to help build police forces, court systems, and legal codes, local and provincial government institutions, and electoral systems. Effective international cooperation is needed to accomplish these goals, backed by American readiness to play our part.

Just as our diplomatic institutions must adapt so that we can reach out to others, we also need a different and more comprehensive approach to public information efforts that can help people around the world learn about and understand America. The war on terrorism is not a clash of civilizations. It does, however, reveal the clash inside a civilization, a battle for the future of the Muslim world. This is a struggle of ideas and this is an area where America must excel.

We will take the actions necessary to ensure that our efforts to meet our global security commitments and protect Americans are not impaired by the potential for investigations, inquiry, or prosecution by the International Criminal Court (ICC), whose jurisdiction does not extend to Americans and which we do not accept. We will work together with other nations to avoid complications in our military operations and cooperation, through such mechanisms as multilateral and bilateral agreements that will protect U.S. nationals from the ICC. We will implement fully the American Servicemembers Protection Act, whose provisions are intended to ensure and enhance the protection of U.S. personnel and officials.

We will make hard choices in the coming year and beyond to ensure the right level and allocation of government spending on national security. The United States Government must strengthen its defenses to win this war. At home, our most important priority is to protect the homeland for the American people.

Today, the distinction between domestic and foreign affairs is diminishing. In a globalized world, events beyond America's borders have a greater impact inside them. Our society must be open to people, ideas, and goods from across the globe. The characteristics we most cherish—our freedom, our cities, our systems of movement, and modern life—are vulnerable to terrorism. This vulnerability will persist long after we bring to justice those responsible for the September 11 attacks. As time passes, individuals may gain access to means of destruction that until now could be wielded only by armies, fleets, and squadrons. This is a new condition of life. We will adjust to it and thrive—in spite of it.

In exercising our leadership, we will respect the values, judgment, and interests of our friends and partners. Still, we will be prepared to act apart when our interests and unique responsibilities require. When we disagree on particulars, we will explain forthrightly the grounds for our concerns and strive to forge viable alternatives. We will not allow such disagreements to obscure our determination to secure together, with our allies and our friends, our shared fundamental interests and values.

Ultimately, the foundation of American strength is at home. It is in the skills of our people, the dynamism of our economy, and the resilience of our institutions. A diverse, modern society has inherent, ambitious, entrepreneurial energy. Our strength comes from what we do with that energy. That is where our national security begins.

Index

About the Contributors

June Teufel Dreyer is Professor and Chair of the Department of Political Science at the University of Miami. Dr. Dreyer is a member of the U.S.–China Economic and Security Review Commission and a Senior Fellow with the Foreign Policy Research Institute. Her research centers on ethnic minorities, the Chinese military, cross-strait relations, and security issues in the Asia–Pacific region. Dr. Dreyer is the author of *China's Forty Millions: Minority Nationalities and National Integration in the People's Republic of China*, and *China's Political System: Modernization and Tradition*. Her articles have appeared in numerous scholarly journals.

Carol Lee Hamrin is a Research Professor at George Mason University and was previously the senior China research specialist at the Department of State. Her current research interests include the development of the nonprofit, nongovernmental sector in China; cultural change, human rights and religious policy; and indigenous resources for conflict management. Her publications include *China and the Challenge of the Future: Changing Political Patterns*, and *Decision-Making in Deng's China: Perspective from Insiders*, coedited with Suisheng Zhao, and articles in *The China Journal* and *ChinaSource Journal*.

Christopher Marsh is Associate Professor of Political Science and Director of Asian Studies at Baylor University. His research centers on communist studies and transition politics, with a focus on Russia and China. He is currently completing a book titled *Unparalleled Reforms: Lesson-Drawing and Policy Choice in the Soviet and Chinese Transitions from Communism*. Dr. Marsh is also the author of *Russia at the Polls: Voters, Elections, and Democratization* and *Making Russian Democracy Work: Social Capital, Economic Development,* *and Democratization*, and numerous journal articles published in *Nationalism and Ethnic Politics,* the *Journal of Baltic Studies,* the *American Journal of Chinese Studies,* and *Communist and Post-Communist Studies.*

Andrew J. Nathan is Class of 1919 Professor of Political Science at Columbia University. His teaching and research interests include Chinese politics and foreign policy, the comparative study of political participation and political culture, and human rights. His current research involves collaborative survey-based studies of political culture and political participation in mainland China, Taiwan, Hong Kong, and other Asian societies. He is the author of numerous books, including *Peking Politics, 1918–1923; Chinese Democracy; China's Crisis; China's Transition; The Great Wall and the Empty Fortress: China's Search for Security* (with Robert S. Ross), and coeditor (with Perry Link), of *The Tiananmen Papers.* His articles have appeared in *World Politics, Daedalus, The China Quarterly, Journal of Democracy, Asian Survey,* and elsewhere.

Minxin Pei is Senior Associate and Codirector of the China Program at the Carnegie Endowment for International Peace. He was previously an Assistant Professor in the Department of Politics at Princeton University, where he taught East Asian politics and international relations. His main interest is the development of democratic political systems, the politics of economic reform, and the growth of civil society and legal institutions. He is completing a book titled *China's Trapped Transition: The Limits of Developmental Autocracy.* Dr. Pei is also the author of *From Reform to Revolution: the Demise of Communism in China and the Soviet Union,* and numerous articles in *Foreign Policy, Foreign Affairs, The National Interest, Modern China, China Quarterly,* and *Journal of Democracy.*

Ambassador J. Stapleton Roy spent forty-five years with the U.S. Department of State before joining Kissinger Associates, Inc., a strategic consulting firm, as Managing Director in 2001. A graduate of Princeton University, he spent much of his career in East Asia, in addition to serving in Moscow at the height of the Cold War. Mr. Roy rose to become a three-time ambassador, serving as the top U.S. envoy in Singapore (1984–1986), the People's Republic of China (1991–1995), and Indonesia (1996–1999). Ambassador Roy's final post with the State Department was as Assistant Secretary for Intelligence and Research.

Strobe Talbott assumed the post of President of the Brookings Institution in July 2002 after a career in journalism, government, and academe. Mr. Talbott served in the State Department from 1993 to 2001, after spending twenty-one years with *Time* magazine. His books include *The Russia Hand: A Memoir of Presidential Diplomacy*, *At the Highest Levels: The Inside Story of the End of the Cold War* (with Michael Beschloss), *Reagan and Gorbachev* (with Michael Mandelbaum), *Deadly Gambits*, and *Reagan and the Russians*, among others. He has also written for *Foreign Affairs*, *The New Yorker*, *Foreign Policy*, *International Security*, *The Economist*, and *The New York Times*.

Suisheng Zhao is Associate Professor at the Graduate School of International Studies and Executive Director of the Center for China–U.S. Cooperation at the University of Denver. He just completed a new book titled *A Nation–State by Construction: Dynamics of Modern Chinese Nationalism*. He is also the author of *Power Competition in East Asia* and editor of *Across the Taiwan Strait* and *China and Democracy*. Dr. Zhao is founding editor of the *Journal of Contemporary China* and his articles have appeared in *Political Science Quarterly*, *The China Quarterly*, *Asian Survey*, *Journal of Democracy*, *Communist and Post-Communist Studies*, and elsewhere.

DATE DUE

FEB 17 2011			
GAYLORD			PRINTED IN U.S.A.